On the Line

ON THE LINE

HARVEY SWADOS

With an Introduction by
Nelson Lichtenstein

University of Illinois Press
Urbana and Chicago

To Bette

Illini Books edition, 1990

© 1957, 1985 by Bette Swados
Introduction © 1990 by the Board of Trustees
of the University of Illinois
Manufactured in the United States of America
1 2 3 4 5 C P 5 4 3 2 1

This book is printed on acid-free paper.

Library of Congress Cataloging-in-Publication Data

Swados, Harvey.
    On the line / Harvey Swados ; with an introduction by Nelson
Lichtenstein. — Illini books ed.
        p. cm.
    Includes bibliographical references.
    Contents: The day the singer fell—Fawn, with a bit of green—
Joe, the vanishing American—A present for the boy—On the line
— One for the road—Just one of the boys—Back in the saddle
again—The myth of the happy worker.
    ISBN 0-252-01674-2 (cloth : alk. paper).—ISBN 0-252-06055-5 (paper :
alk. paper)
    1. Working class—Fiction. I. Title.
PS3569.W205   1990
813'.54—dc20   89-35312
                                                              CIP

Contents

Introduction

NELSON LICHTENSTEIN

We Americans have rediscovered the importance of our work
lives. This might seem rather unsurprising, given the fact
that both sexes are now expected to enter the labor force,
that computers and other machines are opening up opportunities for a transformation of daily labor, that both cor-
porate managers and radical laborites are proposing substantial reform of the workplace. But it was not so long ago
that the meaning of our daily work hardly seemed worth
talking about. In the first quarter century after World War
II, jobs were plentiful, living standards were rising, and if
labor seemed increasingly routine, then automation promised to shrink the workweek; and, perhaps more important,
the bounty of postwar American society—new cars, suburban houses, TV sets and dishwashers—seemed compen-

sation enough for the dullness of the postwar factory and office.

Even the forces of social change hardly questioned the character of work in U.S. factories and offices. "Big labor" might periodically shut down a company for a few weeks, but the most well publicized part of their demands almost always focused on the compensation, not the character, of the work their members did. Even 1960s radicals found it difficult to imagine that most Americans could find creativity and happiness in their work; the New Left's brief infatuation with rural communes and urban self-impoverishment represented more of an escape from than a challenge to the existing order. It was only at the end of that decade that a few of the new radicals began to seriously consider American work life a proper object of reform.

All is different now. To businessmen and women the challenge to American capitalism by Japanese and other competitors has prompted an intense self-scrutiny, extending not just to product development and production technique but to reorganization and motivation of employees, along lines that advance the revitalization of labor in a more efficient workplace. More critically, a new generation of academics, journalists, and labor activists has challenged the notion that our work life must be the product of either the relentless march of new technology or the sophisticated manipulation of a managerial elite. They argue that work is central to the construction of both our politics and our personality, so its history and future are still "contested terrain."

Harvey Swados died in 1972, just as Americans began to rediscover the world of work. But he helped prepare the way. His novels, stories, and spirited reportage in the last decade and a half of his life helped uncover the political and social drama that unfolds in the daily routine of every American workplace. Nothing he wrote accomplished this with more power and insight than the series of interconnected short stories called *On the Line,* which first appeared in the fall of 1957, a book, his wife remembers, that "Harvey dearly loved." This humane and sympathetic portrait of the psychological and social brutality inherent in mid-century factory work injected a moral urgency into the understanding of manual labor at a time, early in the postwar era, when most literary and political intellectuals were convinced that all meaning had been drained from the toil still required of so many millions. As Swados put it in his famous essay "The Myth of the Happy Worker," written just after the publication of *On the Line* and included as an appendix in this edition: "Sooner or later, if we want a decent society—by which I do not mean a society glutted with commodities or one maintained in precarious equilibrium by over-buying and forced premature obsolescence—we are going to have to come face to face with the problem of work. . . . if we cling to the belief that other men are our brothers, . . . including millions of Americans who grind their lives away on an insane treadmill, then we will have to start thinking about how their work and their lives can be made meaningful."[1]

Here Swados prefigures so much that would come later:

the empathic oral histories of Studs Terkel, the labor history of David Montgomery, the journalism of Barbara Garson, and the social psychology of Richard Sennett and Jonathan Cobb. The subtitle of one of the earliest and most influential of these studies, Harry Braverman's *Labor and Monopoly Capital: The Degradation of Work in the Twentieth Century* (1974), reiterates the theme Swados sought to fictionalize in his collection of stories.

Harvey Swados was born in Buffalo, New York, in 1920 of an upper middle-class Russian Jewish family. His father was a physician with many working-class patients; his mother was a singer, pianist, and painter. Coming of age in the 1930s, this sensitive and intelligent youth not unexpectedly turned to radical politics, first as a Communist in high school and later, at the University of Michigan, as a recruit to the Trotskyist movement. At Ann Arbor, Swados enthusiastically followed the dramatic organizing victories of the new auto workers' union, and he participated in an unsuccessful effort to organize the radio factory where he had taken his first industrial job. Swados published several award-winning short stories while at Michigan and even then saw himself primarily as a writer. After his graduation in 1940, however, his political commitments drew him back to Buffalo, where he pounded rivets at Bell Aircraft, passed through a brief first marriage, and then moved on to New York to take another factory job in the big, turbulent Brewster Aviation plant in Long Island City, just across the East River from Manhattan.[2]

During these years, Swados gave his allegiance to the Workers' party, a small but extremely energetic and resourceful political group whose adherents he would later describe in *Standing Fast,* his 1970 novel that sympathetically recorded the exhilaration and despair of his political generation as it moved from the radical hopes of the late 1930s to a kind of acquiescent liberalism in the 1950s and 1960s. Despite his own drift away from the revolutionary expectations of his youth, much that would remain central to Swados's world view was formed in these politically charged years of factory employment in the early 1940s.

An anti-Stalinist radical, Swados rejected the Soviet Union as any kind of model for the society he hoped to build. Instead, he—and others committed to his brand of Trotskyist politics—put their faith in a militant, international working class that would stand as a "third camp" opposed to the ruling classes in both capitalist and communist regimes. To put their ideas into practice, they took factory jobs in the booming war plants of Detroit, Chicago, Buffalo, and New York. Here they defended the wildcat strikes that periodically erupted, pushed for a labor party, and attacked those in the labor movement, such as the Communists, who subordinated working-class aspirations for a better life and a more democratic workplace to the foreign policy interests of one of the big powers. The Workers' party had but a slight impact on the politics of American labor, but this wartime experience profoundly affected many in the generation of students and intellectuals who had "industrialized" in those years. For Swados, the imprint of such politics remained in his sensitivity to the psychology of everyday work and in the unsentimental way he identified with the oppressed and the enthusiasm with which he greeted the struggles of blacks and students in the 1960s. Until his premature death of an aneurysm at age fifty-two, Swados counted himself a socialist and a radical.

Politics aside, Swados found life in the wartime factories and in his tightly disciplined radical sect confining. At Brewster, production was chaotic, the hours too long, and the boredom stupefying. So he did what thousands of young men had done for generations: he escaped to the sea, joining the merchant marine in 1943 as a radio operator and then traveling around the world, sometimes in dangerous waters. Returning to New York in 1946, he married Bette Beller and bought a house in Rockland County, twenty miles north of Manhattan. Between 1947 and 1955, Swados wrote furiously. Several short stories and a well-received novel, *Out Went the Candle* (1955), which focused on the family of a Jewish businessman who became a war profiteer in the 1940s, were published during this period.[3]

Finding time to write and to earn a living was always difficult. For a while Swados wrote and did public relations for Israel bonds. He also wrote for television, in the process developing a lifelong animosity toward low-brow culture. In the mid-1950s he took his wife and three small children to the south of France, where a friend gave them a rent-free house, but he failed to finish his big novel of American life there. In need of work upon his return to New York, Swados found his efforts to land a college teaching job or win a writing fellowship unsuccessful. But he was nonetheless loathe to return to the world of speech writing and public relations—a world for which he had never had much sympathy, even when he worked in the middle of it.[4]

Fifteen miles from his home, the Ford Motor Company had just finished constructing the largest automobile assembly plant in the world, in Mahwah, New Jersey. This sprawling, single-story factory, big enough to cover seven football fields under a single roof, employed more than 3,500 workers on two shifts. Built as part of Ford's gigantic postwar expansion and modernization plan, the new Mahwah factory was designed to turn out 800 Fords and Mercurys and 250 Ford trucks each eight-hour shift. Like the other eighteen assembly plants Ford ran in the 1950s, the Mahwah facility contained no computers or robots, but Ford engineers had designed every part of the factory to ensure the most efficient and continuous production regime. The main building had ten miles of fifteen-foot-wide aisles, five miles of overhead conveyors, and two and a half miles of ground-floor assembly lines. A ninety-foot-wide runway for a double railroad track ran right under the forty-acre roof; outside, the parking lot had space for 5,500 cars.[5] In *On the Line* Swados described the plant as a "vast, endless, steel and concrete world" through which "an endless succession of auto bodies slowly and inexorably" rolled past the workers "like so many faceless steel robots."

When Swados showed up at the Mahwah plant in February 1956, the personnel man was glad to see that he had had some blue-collar work experience, but he also found his job application strangely full of blank spots. When asked what he had been doing, Swados dodged: "Writing novels in the south of France." This little joke seemed to satisfy, so he was promptly assigned to the assembly line as a metal finisher, the same job he had mastered in the early 1940s when working in Buffalo. Some years later Swados remembered the shock of his return to factory labor: "I was appalled all over again but also tremendously excited, a selfish excitement because I said to myself, 'Good Lord, here they are! I have forgotten all about them. They have been here all these years, making all of these things, and here I am with them, but now I know what it is all about.' "[6]

Metal finishing is one of the more skilled production jobs on an assembly line. It requires a certain judgment and technique with a hammer and file. But the work is also exhausting, the hours long. Swados lost seventeen pounds in a couple of months, and by April he reported his right hand "crippled up from pushing a file against steel ten hours a night." However, he was excited as the idea of a new collection of short stories framed around the metal finishing line of the body shop took shape. He talked with his work-mates, took down their life stories, and told them he was a writer. They called him "Shakespeare."

"Everything has fallen into place for me," Swados wrote after two months on the job. "My earlier factory years have meaning now that they didn't before, and I think now I really know the pity and the vanity of American life from the inside." Writing a page or two each day before he set off for work on the night shift, Swados became increasingly enthusiastic about the collection. The stories were his best work yet: "I think when they are all done they will give an inkling of what has happened to the American dream. Even their titles are good!"[7]

Swados punched in at Mahwah at a time when many people saw the very existence of an American working class as up for grabs. The Census Bureau had just reported that for the first time in U.S. history the number of clerical, sales, and service ("white-collar") workers outnumbered those who worked in factories, mines, and construction sites ("blue-collar"). Moreover, with the demise of industrial violence, the steady increase in real wages, and the tidal wave of consumer goods available even to factory hands, the once-alien, politically charged character of the industrial working class seemed at an end. As *Fortune* put it in 1951, the misery and conflict of the Great Depression now belonged to a remote, barely believable past. Then, observed the influential business magazine, "bloodshed and hate stalked the streets of Gadsden, Toledo, Detroit and Aliquippa. Looking back . . . these memories seem almost incredible."[8]

Thanks to the success of the unions and to a pragmatic, enlightened management, class divisions had been reduced in the postwar years to virtual irrelevance. "We have no classes in this country," trade union leader Philip Murray boldly told a convention of the once-radical Congress of Industrial Organizations, "that's why the Marxist theory of the class struggle has gained so few adherents. . . . the interests of farmers, factory hands, business and professional people, and white collar toilers prove to be the same."[9] The union, wrote the editors of *Fortune,* "has made the worker to an amazing degree a middle-class member of a middle-class society—in the plant, in the local community, in the economy."[10] Or, as Swados himself put it, explaining this viewpoint in "The Myth of the Happy Worker," "if the worker earns like the middle-class, votes like the middle-class, dresses like the middle-class, dreams like the middle-class, then he ceases to exist as a worker."[11]

Indeed, workers as *workers* seemed on the verge of disappearance from the public imagination. Sociologist David Riesman's widely read *The Lonely Crowd* (1950) summarized much contemporary social science wisdom, arguing that with the shift from "an age of production to an age of consumption," work had ceased to be a central experience in the lives of American men and women. With craftsmanship in decline and production unproblematic, Americans had progressed to a point at which the "inner-directed" personality would give way to an "other-directed" personhood focused on the manipulation of symbols and people in a world of declining labor and greater leisure. Historian David Potter extended Riesman's argument in *People of Plenty: Economic Abundance and the American Character* (1954), arguing that consumption and the ability to collect it were not just recent phenomena but the defining characteristics of American life.[12]

Auto workers partook fully in this postwar sense of affluence. They were among the best paid of all American workers in the mid-1950s, and their union, the United Auto Workers, was without doubt the most powerful and imaginatively led of all labor institutions. Under the skillful leadership of ex-Socialist Walter Reuther, the UAW had negotiated higher wages, company-paid pensions and health insurance, and in 1955 a supplemental income scheme designed to provide workers with a substantial portion of their income even if they were laid off. UAW members were buying tract houses, taking vacations, and agitating for more parking space in factory lots. Most important, the union had curbed the unfettered power of the shop bosses, bringing a measure of due process and industrial justice to the resolution of the daily conflicts that inevitably broke out on the shop floor of the thousand or more workplaces in which the UAW held bargaining rights.

Appearing in the midst of this celebration of American life, *On the Line* became—and still is—a powerful argument for the continued existence of an American working class. Despite high levels of consumption, unionization, and political complacency, Swados would later write, "there is one thing that the worker doesn't do like the middle-class: he works like a worker."[13] Swados thus returned his readers to one of Karl Marx's most important insights, namely, that class is not defined by income or consumption level but by the relationship to the means of production, to the authority vested in those who own capital, and to subordination of the many to the authority of the few.

On the Line drives this point home in a series of eight short stories, each moving a different worker under the authorial spotlight, with a number of characters appearing shadowlike in two or three stories. There is no single protagonist, although Swados's story of Walter—the young, awkward, metal finisher who is pounding and sweating his way toward college—has a clear autobiographical ring, as does his portrait of the itinerant radical named Joe. This old Wobbly, this "Vanishing American," becomes Walter's mentor, offering him a credo that would also guide Swados as a reporter and critic of industrial America: "Never mind the machinery. Remember the men. The men make the machines and they make their own tragedies too."

Indeed, these stories are full of tragedy, and not a little pathos as well. The first opens with LeRoy (significantly, none of the characters have full names), a powerful black with a golden voice who works only to earn money to continue his vocal studies. As with his other characters, Swados describes LeRoy's work routine in precise and telling detail. As "hook man," he has to jump on the auto bodies as they move past him and clamp each one with a heavy steel hook and chain so that it can be hoisted to the soldering booth. The work is "hard, dull, unremitting and backbreaking." Still, LeRoy believes in the American Dream. "They don't even know your name here, only your social security number and your time clock number," he tells a workmate. But he looks forward to an escape, to the day when everyone will know his name after he successfully auditions for the Metropolitan Opera. Of course, that day never comes: LeRoy slips on a row of moving bodies and his neck strikes an open swinging door. He never sings again.

Other dreams are shattered as well. Kevin is a young Irish immigrant, the proud owner of an emerald green convertible built right on his line, a country schoolteacher who is first astonished, even pleased, by the "vast, endless steel and concrete world" in which he works. But this magical ambience soon fades as Kevin grows familiar with the plant and contemplates a lifetime of car payments and rent bills that would "chain him to the line for years." The automobile as a seductive but corrupting consumer product is also present in the story of Pop, a widower nearing retirement who sinks most of his savings into a muscle car built right on the Ford factory assembly line. It's a present for his son, Rudy, a newly minted high school graduate upon whom Pop pours his hopes and vanities. But like the work that built it, this product of the factory is self-destructive, ending Rudy's life in a drunken Saturday night smash-up.

Orrin and Harold have few illusions. They are embittered and disappointed men who find a kind of solace in the challenge of the assembly line. But hardworking Orrin is ultimately humiliated by his physical inability to keep up with the pace, while Harold, once a talented commercial

artist, can keep his alcoholism at bay only through unremitting and purposeless toil.

Finally, Swados offers a commentary on management and
the union in his portraits of Buster, the foreman, and Frank,
an older anti-union auto worker who escaped the factory in
his youth only to return there after repeated failures in business. Buster had once been "one of the boys," but as foreman
he now finds himself squeezed painfully between the higher-
level supervisors and college-educated engineers above and
the seemingly irresponsible gang of sixteen assembly line
workers for whose work he remains responsible. Buster sees
himself as fair-minded and helpful—he values the good
opinion of his men—but he has to keep his psychological
distance. When production gets tight, he has to crack down,
if only to protect his own hopes for a promotion. Like other
foremen, and like the workers themselves, he is a victim of
a system of authority and technology that not only controls
his physical movements but reshapes his soul.

In the closing episode, Swados shows how Frank, deeply
humiliated by his return to factory work and his dependence
on the union he once hated, reconciles himself to his new
station in life. Frank realizes that things are different from
before, the line moves slower, the fear and dog-eat-dog ten-
sion are gone. "I feel a little funny coming back after all this
time to ride the gravy train," he tells his wife. When he is
faced with an unexpected layoff, a final disastrous humiliation, the "union boys" save Frank's job and treat him with
unexpected kindness and respect at the weekend picnic of

the United Auto Workers' local. Frank's committeeman persuades plant personnel that Frank's seniority in the factory should count for something. "We got no legal right. But they got to live with us like we got to live with them," the unionist tells Frank and his once-skeptical wife. It's a "little victory," a bit of class collaboration, but it restores some of Frank's dignity and seals his reconciliation with the union.

Compared with the other stories, unrelenting in their harsh portrayal of the factory world, Frank's episode is the only one that seems sentimental. As a conclusion to the collection, Swados makes an implicit comparison between Frank's union-assisted "little victory" and the outright defeat and frustration that is the lot of most of the other characters. Even Joe, the clear-eyed radical, disappears after planting with Walter the insights the young man will need to understand what is happening to his fellow workers. But Swados's point is that the union is here to stay. It can't revolutionize the factory, but it does stand for fair play and openheartedness—something to value in the moral chaos of Ford's assembly line.

Swados revealed himself to be very much an intellectual of the 1950s—aware of injustice but incapable of pointing toward any fundamental resolution. In his emphasis on the alienation of modern work, rather than on the simultaneous possibilities for self-liberation, he shared much of the despair of such equally radical social critics as C. Wright Mills, his neighbor and friend, who even more than Swados came to see the American working class as essentially a powerless victim. The frustration of modern work can therefore rarely be translated into anything more than a cry from the heart.

But Swados overlooked something important at Mahwah: the inchoate solidarities and social norms workers themselves create in even the most oppressive employment situations. This work culture, which arises organically out of the interplay between the natural rhythms of the work process and the ethnic and generational composition of the work force, can provide a powerful basis for resistance and organization. The union picnic Swados described in *On the Line* offers a glimpse of such fraternity, but it is a pale vision of the solidarity that is episodically forged out of shop floor friendships and struggle.

Swados missed this, in part because he wasn't looking for it, but also because circumstances prevented him from full immersion in a rich factory work life. He was at Mahwah for less than a year, and he lived not in one of the working-class neighborhoods of northern New Jersey but in the more rural, small-town groves of Rockland County, New York. More important, perhaps, the Mahwah plant had just opened in a social wilderness at the confluence of two recently completed freeways. Although many workers had come from an older Ford plant in Edgewater, most of those on the less-desirable night shift where Swados worked were new to the factory, without the friendships and social contacts that would inevitably weave their dense web throughout the plant. "The absenteeism was fantastic," remembered Swados shortly after he quit. "You could never be sure of enough men to keep the line rolling except on payday."[14] All this meant that, despite his keen powers of observation, his brief sojourn in the plant did not give him the time or the opportunity to fully discover the informal networks that almost always arise to texture the work lives of most blue-collar workers.[15]

Mahwah workers would in fact demonstrate a combativeness that was not atypical of auto workers in this prosperous era. Like other auto workers, Mahwah unionists, organized into UAW Local 906, were engaged in a constant fight over the pace and content of their work. As early as December 1957, 80 percent of the local's membership voted to strike Ford if their numerous grievances over the company's violation of the health and safety provisions of the contract and over work standards—the amount of sheer physical labor each worker must put into his job—were not resolved.[16] Local 906 easily shut down the plant when the UAW struck the Ford Motor Company in 1958, 1961, 1964, and 1967. But workers also "wildcatted" without going through the UAW's formal strike procedures. In July 1959, 178 workers walked out of the trim department to protest company efforts to discipline a union committeeman. Two years later, 2,000 workers shut down the entire plant during a September heat wave that drove temperatures above 90° inside sections of the plant. Then in November 1962, all 4,350 members of Local 906 participated in an officially sanctioned strike over eighty-three unresolved grievances, many involving safety problems.[17]

Swados became loosely attached to the academy in the

late 1950s, but he maintained his interest in the labor movement and the world of work. For many years he taught at Sarah Lawrence and the University of Massachusetts at Amherst. His writing classes frequently visited the factory districts and union halls of New York and Boston. He was extremely productive, publishing two more novels, *False Coin* (1959) and *The Will* (1963), as well as stories, anthologies, and a biography of Estes Kefauver, *Standing Up for the People* (1972). Although he considered himself first and foremost a novelist, he had also become an experienced labor journalist, publishing long essays on the difficulties that mechanization had brought to coal miners and longshoremen. His 1958 essay, "The Myth of the Powerful Worker," challenged the conventional wisdom that equated "big labor" with "big business." Many of his labor essays were collected in *A Radical's America* (1962), which enjoyed currency within the early New Left.

In one of his most important and controversial essays of the early 1960s, "The UAW—Over the Top or Over the Hill?" Swados returned to the condition of workers and their union in the auto industry. But in this 1963 investigation of what happened to the once-radical UAW, he was far more critical of the union than he had been in *On the Line.* Here, the alienation, humiliation, and speed-up experienced by automobile workers were seen less as the product of industrial life itself than as a consequence of the UAW's failure to fulfill the aspirations of its founding generation. Confronted with the financial and political strength of the most powerful

American corporations, the UAW tempered its fight against job dissatisfaction, unemployment, and racial discrimination. Swados recognized that Walter Reuther was by far the most imaginative and progressive of contemporary trade union leaders, but in a critique of the Reuther circle that a generation of New Leftists would later make of other liberals, he declared that the union leadership hardly took its own reformist demands seriously anymore. Manipulation therefore replaced mobilization of the membership, and bureaucracy triumphed over locally initiated activism.[18]

At Mahwah itself, conflict between a liberal union and a radicalized section of the rank and file became increasingly manifest during the late 1960s and early 1970s. By the end of the decade the plant was more than half African American. Inspired by the civil rights and black power movements sweeping so much of this community, black workers in the plant organized a brief but militant insurgency. A new group, the United Black Brotherhood of Ford Mahwah, attacked the local's white union leadership for its failure to defend black workers, and the group sparked strikes and walkouts for dignity and civil treatment in 1969. Much to the alarm of UAW officials, the Brotherhood on one occasion invited radicals from the Black Panther party and Students for a Democratic Society to assist in picketing the plant.

Writing in the *New York Times,* Swados applauded the student-worker collaboration, seeing "signs that some students . . . are ridding themselves of glib anti-union attitudes and coming to the factories in search of allies, rather than

simply as hip leafleteers on another kind of trip." Furthermore, he argued, their potential alliance raised the question
with which he had struggled since the publication of *On the
Line:* "If universities are to be humanized, why not factories
and offices?"[19] The issue remains unresolved. But like so
much of Harvey Swados's writing, the questions he posed
command a moral response from all those who work or who
know something of work's meaning.

NOTES

1. See p. 247, this volume. The essay was first published in *The
Nation,* August 17, 1957.

2. For more on Swados, see Alan Wald, *The New York Intellectuals:
The Rise and Decline of the Anti-Stalinist Left from the 1930s to the
1980s.* Chapel Hill: University of North Carolina Press, 1987, 334-
39.

3. Ibid., 335.

4. Swados's efforts to earn a living are recounted in Harvey Swados, "Some Social Implications of Automation," ms. dated April 19,
1966, box 23, Swados Collection, University of Massachusetts; and
in a Lichtenstein telephone interview with Robin Swados, July 25,
1989.

5. "First Ford Rolls in Mahwah Plant," *New York Times,* July 17,
1955.

6. Quoted in U.S. Department of Labor, "Seminar on Manpower
Policy and Program," box 23, Swados Collection.

7. Harvey Swados to Stuart and Barbara Schulberg, April 5, 1956,
box 33, Swados Collection.

8. Quoted in Russell Davenport, *USA: The Permanent Revolution.*
New York: Time-Life, 1951, 91.

9. *Proceedings,* Congress of Industrial Organizations, November
1948, 234.

10. Quoted in Davenport, 91.

11. See p. 237, this volume.

12. For further discussion, see Jeffrey Halprin, "Getting Back to Work: The Revaluation of Work in American Literature and Social Theory, 1950-1985." Ph.D. diss., Boston University, 1987, 46-52.

13. See p. 237, this volume.

14. Harvey Swados, *A Radical's America.* New York: World Publishing, 1962, 118.

15. Lichtenstein telephone interview with Stan Weir, October 14, 1988.

16. "Ford Strike Is Voted," *New York Times,* December 11, 1957.

17. "Ford Workers Quit," *New York Times,* September 6, 1961; "Ford Mahwah Plant Halted by Walkout," *New York Times,* November 28, 1962.

18. Harvey Swados, "The UAW—Over the Top or Over the Hill?" *Dissent,* Fall 1963, 321-43.

19. "Topics: Workers and Students—Enemies or Allies?" *New York Times,* August 30, 1969. Unfortunately, Ford Motor Company had the last laugh. Complaining of poor workmanship, it permanently closed down the big factory in the summer of 1980.

On the Line

ONE

The Day the Singer Fell

LEROY was an easygoing but prideful man, never one to look for trouble but sure of what he wanted from life, uniting openly in his person the self-respect that had been carefully buried in his father and the belief in human goodness always adhered to by his mother. His father, a tall, stern, and enormously powerful mulatto, had worked all his life waiting on table at the naval officers' mess in the Norfolk yards; his mother still lived by what she earned at home as a seamstress. Together, they had managed to give LeRoy two and a half years at Hampton Institute before his mother needed his earning power, and it was at Hampton that LeRoy found himself.

He was singing in the shower one afternoon, after a late workout in the gym (he was a big man on the freshman basketball and track teams), and a visiting professor of music happened to hear him through the open window. Within a week he had become a member of the Hampton Choir; within the month he had discovered his true ambition. Thereafter the glamor of athletics paled beside a new vision of power and success. Quickly, with an almost fatally desperate urgency, he made the change-over to the music and language courses he now knew he must have. Yet even when his father began to fade before his eyes from an insidious lung cancer (unfortunately not listed by the Navy as a service-connected disability) and LeRoy had at last to drop out of school, he was wretched, but he did not look upon the family disaster as anything more than a detour, certainly not a derailment, from the track leading to his chosen goal.

When he sat in the office of the man who had first heard his voice, and waited passively, big hands folded over his textbooks, for the professor to finish typing three letters of recommendation to friends in New York, LeRoy did not even feel depressed. Beneath his stolidity he was itching to be off.

"LeRoy," the professor said almost plaintively, as he slipped the brief letters into their envelopes and passed them across his desk, "I have great hopes for you." He was a white man, pale, freckled, earnest, and now he leaned forward tentatively, almost frightenedly, and put his hand on LeRoy's forearm.

"You've got a golden throat," he said.

LeRoy lowered his head in embarrassment.

"Take care of it. In five years, maybe seven, eight . . . Drop me a line."

LeRoy took the letters and the memory to New York. With their help he was accepted by a voice teacher, who also got him some Sunday work in church choirs. He took a room on One-hundred-and-forty-third Street in the basement apartment of the building's supervisor, whose assistant he became, and he got extra jobs stoking furnaces in neighboring houses which had not yet converted to automatic or gas. But as he wrote to his mother, he felt like he was treading water instead of swimming — he wasn't making enough to send her home a decent check, his hours were too irregular for continuous voice study and practice, and besides, there was his girl friend Lily.

She was a niece of the lady in whose apartment he lived and, although she was a trained stenotypist, worked as a bookkeeper in a big furniture store on One-hundred-and-twenty-fifth Street. LeRoy was shy with her when they first met. He had found out quickly enough that the slick Harlem chicks were completely unimpressed by small-town boys, even when the boys wore track letters on their sweaters, and without the athletic line that had worked on the girls back at Hampton he was a little frightened. But she was beautiful, she smelled sweet as a flower, and she was no dough-blowing fly-by-night, so in desperation he started to confide in her. In a week they were taking long walks on the hard sand at Jones Beach, and in three months she promised to marry him.

Dazed by his good fortune, LeRoy was inclined to think that what did it was having Lily with him at church choir practice, where she sat staring dumbly from a deserted pew while he smiled down at her and raised his voice joyously.

"LeRoy, you've got it, you've really got it!" she cried as soon as they were out on the street. She hugged his arm. "You've got a golden throat, just like that man said."

"Ah, stop it." He half regretted having told Lily the professor's parting words. "There's a million like me. Never realized it till I came up here."

"Don't ever lose your nerve, man. I'm never going to give up on that throat, and don't you do it either. LeRoy, LeRoy, let's never get all sour and mean. Let's be lovers."

So they went to City Hall and he moved into the flat where Lily lived with her stepmother, three smaller brothers, her stepmother's uncle-in-law, and a schoolteacher lodger, and he started to look for other work. It had to be real money, enough to take care of regular voice lessons, and of Lily, whose baby was already growing within her — for she had not denied him and he did not honestly feel that he could deny her.

"I'm willing to bust my hump for some walking-around money," he said to his friend Teddy, a lanky, cigar-chewing black man who was hacking out of a stand on Lenox Avenue. "Just lead me to it. I got more muscles than you ever heard of. And I got reasons for working hard."

Teddy chewed thoughtfully. "I got an application in at the new auto assembly plant upstate. No money driving a hack, except Saturday nights, and I can still do that if they hire me. Ever do factory work?"

"There's no work I can't do." LeRoy laughed proudly. "You know how powerful my lungs are? My back is just as strong. I want to put my back to work for my lungs, you know what I mean? And for my Lily."

"Listen, boy, don't get thinking you can whip the whole world. They got jobs to break a man's back — or his heart — that you never even heard about down where you come from."

Sobered, LeRoy opened his clenched hands and said to the older man, "You say this place is upstate. How you going to get there every day?"

"Car pool. If I get four riders at a buck and a half a head round trip, it covers the payments on my new Mercury."

LeRoy made the first trip by bus, stood in line, filled out forms, and was hired. Teddy too had been hired, had posted a notice on the bulletin board at Gate 2, and had acquired two more passengers, Irish boys from uptown whom he picked up at their street corner en route. For LeRoy, riding in the same car (even when he was in front with Teddy and they sat in back) with these fast-talking, wisecracking Northern white boys, who seemed interested only in girls, beer, and cars and who scarcely seemed to notice the fact that he and Teddy were Negroes, was a far stranger experience than the huge new factory itself.

The work was hard, dull, unremitting, and backbreaking. Behind his smiling jollity and his eagerness to be friends with everyone, LeRoy was often dark with frustration and impotence. If it had been possible, he would have preferred working on the waterfront in the fresh air with Italians who sang and Puerto Ricans who laughed, where he too could sing at his work and fill his lungs with air. In the factory — which otherwise he accepted as he accepted without thinking the dirt, noise, poverty, and excitement of the city — he felt that his lungs were being choked with dust and his spirit with mindless monotony, and that in order to get the money he now had to have, it was necessary for him to put in long hours of overtime that he might better have spent with his wife or his music. It weighed on him, too, that aside from Teddy there was no one in the plant in whom he could confide, no one with whom he could drop what was developing into his LeRoy-the-Nut act — until Kevin the Irishman turned up and was assigned to be his partner.

They worked together in the body shop as hook men, clambering up on each auto body as it glided past to clamp onto it twenty-pound hooks and chains, so that when it reached the end of the line it could be swung in the air by the hooks like a huge side of beef and hoisted high into the bonderizing booth. The hooks and chains returned by overhead conveyer, coated with rustproofing primer, and LeRoy was always covered, from the bill of his baseball cap to the steel toes of his high-top shoes, with their red dust, which sometimes lay across his cheeks and forehead too when he paused to wipe his face with the back of his glove. Not only the primer but the poisonous dust which lay on the air from the equipment of the solderers, metal finishers, and fitters working on the bodies as they moved along the assembly line was intensely irritating to LeRoy. From time to time he put on a small mask which he had requisitioned from the tool crib. It fitted neatly over his nose and had a little rubber bladder for breathing through the mouth, but it did not quite cover his smile.

LeRoy was well aware that this was going to get him talked about. It was not like wearing goggles to protect the eyes, which was practical; protecting your throat, as he explained to Lily, seemed sissyish. "But I can't be all the time worrying about what people will think," he said. "I don't get paid for that. As long as I do my work."

"As long as you take care of your throat," Lily replied, touching his feet under the table with hers. They were having some ribs at a tavern she liked; it was Saturday night, and for the moment the weariness of the long week — they had both worked all day Saturday — was forgotten. "I don't care about that old job, just because you make big money. It's the future that counts. If they don't like how you do in that factory, tell them to go to hell, LeRoy."

LeRoy told no one to go to hell. He had never done that in his life. He truly enjoyed being polite to people, and even making them laugh, and someplace at the bottom of his mind lay the notion that one day he would be able to do even more for them than that. But he could not help being blue when he thought (and what else was there to do in the body shop except think about the same things all day?)

about what his life would be like if he did not have the musical career to look forward to: it was terrifying, just the thought of being stuck here forever with no hope of escape, and it drove him to study harder, just as the fear of what happened to thieves had kept him from fooling with his mother's purse when he was a small boy.

He didn't really want to hide those blues, whenever they gripped him by the throat, any more than he did the mask that he put over his mouth when the dust grew too thick — or the big voice that he couldn't keep muffled all the time, but had to let go with whenever things were going good and the future looked exciting. Still, at those moments when he had to withdraw into himself, he rode the line, squatting in the trunk compartment of a metal skeleton, hiding from the foreman and all the deadly world under the upraised deck lid and cupping his only solace in the palm of his thick, red-stained glove, and at least no one could see the blues riding on his back. And if that was the dark side of his being that no one actually knew of, not even Lily, then the light side was the natural laughter with which he responded to gags and kidding, the habit he had of turning to the world the soft grin which he honestly preferred — not, like his father, as a painfully acquired obsequiousness, but as an expression of his belief in the goodness of most people. The blues, he felt, were only a sign of his own occasional uncertainty about his future; what was really basic to his own view was love and confidence.

So he sang as he worked, sang at the top of his lungs, opening his mouth so wide that he could see reflected in the passing bodies of glittering steel not only his eyeball-white teeth, but the pink palate beyond. He didn't care what the men said, the men or the white-shirted bosses; he opened up with scales, spirituals, and arias in a voice big enough to compete — even though he himself could barely hear what he was singing, and the men about him could make out the sounds but not the refrain — with air hammers, pneumatic drills, hissing flow guns that could throw three feet of spitting blue-red flame, warning horns of swaying trucks carrying spare parts down the aisles, and the grinding clank of the assembly line itself. Then the sweating men around him, looking up dazedly from their endless work at this alien sound too big for the kind of singing to which they were accustomed, would begin to shake their heads at each other significantly, to grin in pity for themselves at what they had to endure, and finally, led by the youngsters on the line, to groan, bay, and howl like wolves in agony.

Some called him Caruso, or Mario Lanza; others wanted to know if he thought he was Hitler or Napoleon; and there were some who seriously asked him what the hell he thought he was doing. LeRoy responded with good humor, agreeing mildly with those who dismissed him as a happy-go-lucky nut, resisting just as mildly the attempts of others to ask personal questions about his singing, and telling those few who brashly demanded to know what he did with the dingus he cupped in the palm of his glove: "That's my secret weapon, man, my Pied Piper tool, boy. When I'm good and ready I'm going to blow it strong and blow it loud, and I'm going to call every last one of you off this dirty old assembly line and out into the sunshine where you belong!"

Only his partner Kevin, who hung the front hooks, license-plate holders, and station-wagon doors, learned what it was that LeRoy hid in his palm — and what it was, for that matter, that LeRoy stared at in his open toolbox in his free moments. LeRoy wanted badly to be completely free from outside involvement with the men on the line, but he found that he could not resist this Irishman fresh off the boat, with his funny voice that had its own kind of music, his eager curiosity not just about LeRoy but about everything, his uncombed shock of almost orange hair, and his great harmless bulk, which towered even over LeRoy.

When Kevin asked, burning with the desire to know, "Tell me now, LeRoy, what is that little thing you're always puttin' to your lips?" he simply had to be answered.

"Well now, I'll tell you, boy," LeRoy responded. "I've been practicing my solfeggio, that's what."

"There's a lovely word. But what does it mean?"

LeRoy thumped down the heavy hook and chain he had picked up from the dolly beside them. "Jesus, don't they teach you people nothing in County Kerry?"

"It's nearly two hundred miles from Dublin, you know," Kevin replied with humility. "But we were always musical nonetheless. Many's the evening I've wound up the gram to play our O'Sullivan records for the folks."

"The fighter?"

"No, no, this one was a grand singer."

"Never heard of him, boy," LeRoy said flatly. "Not that I doubt your word, or claim to know all the great ones. You sing much at home, before you set out to see the world?"

"Just in the choir of St. Malachy's."

"Ah. I've done that too." LeRoy suddenly laughed gaily. "But you like to open up once in a while, and you can't do that in a choir, right? For me, it's like owning a racing car and never being able to run it faster than thirty-five."

"I can see that." Kevin nodded. His plume of bright hair bobbed up and down over the high freckled dome of his forehead. "But what's about this solfeggio?"

"That's my practice in singing notes, different scales and so on, in exact tune. Now this little widget here" — LeRoy took the small shiny disc from the upper pocket of his coveralls — "has got all the notes marked on it like a harmonica, engraved right in, you see, F, F sharp, et cetera. I just blow on it a little from one time to another so as I know where I am. Then I can just go ahead and open her up and let those hyenas howl." And he laughed once again, throwing back his head as he hopped up blithely onto the moving line and swung his hook into place.

He and Kevin had taken up too much time with their talk, however, and had fallen behind, getting in the way of the men at the end of the line who were feverishly busy

with final clean-up. The conveyer rose as it reached its
end, like a gently banked roller coaster, until it reached a
waist-high, metal-cleated dead-end, after which the cars
swung gently free, suspended from the hooks and chains
which LeRoy and Kevin had attached to them. Buster the
foreman rolled his cigar to the corner of his mouth and spat
a stream of brown juice at LeRoy's feet.

"Get your job done up the line where you're supposed
to," he shouted. He added irrelevantly, but with pent-up
fury, "God damned baritone!"

"I'm not a —" LeRoy started as he jumped nimbly off
the line and stepped over the tangle of hoses at his feet; but
Buster had already turned his back. LeRoy shrugged,
chuckled, raised his hands helplessly to his grinning fellow
workers, muttered very low, "Man doesn't even know a
tenor from a baritone," and began to sing once again.

It was not until later in the week, while he was standing
before his open toolbox, polishing his goggles with a soft
rag for the benefit of any passing supervisors, and glancing
occasionally into the box, that LeRoy felt the great shadow
of Kevin at his shoulder. He turned swiftly and bumped into
the Irishman's massive chest.

"Sorry."

"Sorry."

"Say now, listen, man," Kevin nudged, all unabashed,
"what is it that you're always peeking at there? What is it
that you're after?"

LeRoy raised his powerful arm from the edge of the toolbox and disclosed the mimeographed sheets that lay folded within like paper napkins.

"It's no secret," he said plainly. "I'm studying music, and I just don't want the bosses on my tail. The rest of the men, they know enough when they hear me sing. I keep some of my lessons in here so as to learn a little extra. Then I do my solfeggio too, and the time passes that way."

Kevin gazed at him, marveling. Everything that the Irishman was thinking, it seemed to LeRoy, lay as open on his face as his national origin and his character: that he was still unused to black men, just as he was unused to this huge factory and its cacophony of unimagined noises; and that he could not understand why it was that Americans seemed only amused by Negroes, or disgusted by them, when to him the black man — so like himself and yet apparently so different — was a creature of wonder.

He said slowly, "So it's really a singer you're going to be? Like in the opera halls?"

LeRoy answered very seriously, "Every man ought to have an aim. Maybe in your country it's different, but here you're nothing without an aim. They don't even know your name here, only your social security number and your time clock number. If I didn't have the singing to think about, if I didn't have anything to look forward to except eight hours more of this tomorrow, I believe I'd get old before my time. That's why I say you got to have an aim."

Kevin folded his arms and tilted his head. "A name, you say? Or an aim?"

"Something to shoot for, that's what. Take me. I expect one day I'm going to be on the Metropolitan Opera Auditions of the Air. I fully expect it."

"I don't know that show. Comes night and I prowl the town, or write my letters home. It must be a big one, that program."

"Gives you a big chance." LeRoy slammed his box shut. "You sing one or two arias, maybe a duet with a soprano contestant. And if you got the stuff, you get your break — they sign you up to an opera contract. Even without that, there's millions of people listening, so even if the Metropolitan don't want you, you're bound to be heard by somebody else that might."

Kevin looked at him with his mouth open. "Just like that? An ordinary workingman, they'll pick you to stand up before that microphone and perform for the delight of millions?"

LeRoy pursed his lips and spoke more cautiously. "Well, I understand you got to be recommended. My regular teacher, he's not big enough, but he knows another teacher that is — only I can't afford his price. That's why I keep on practicing, maybe he'll give me a scholarship. It's happened before, why not to me?"

"Sure, and why not?" Kevin said encouragingly.

Now he knew why LeRoy wore the mask, and blew on the little birdcall, but the answer to those questions only seemed to call up others. LeRoy was positive that Kevin wondered now why he worked on the assembly line at all, when he might have done something paying less but relating more to his true ambition. It was only a matter of time until Kevin would work up the courage to ask; and finally he did.

"Because I've got a pregnant wife, that's why." LeRoy laughed happily. "She's going to make me a daddy and I'm going to make her some money."

This too was something none of the other men had known. LeRoy had been satisfied to have them think of him as queer and comical, a bellowing buffoon who could hardly be growing into a responsible family man.

LeRoy continued with his singing and the men continued with their baying. He gave them, he knew, one of their few common distractions from the quick exhausting drudgery of their work, but no one knew how much his voice had become a part of the long day on the line until the day he fell.

He was behindhand in his job, far behind, this Monday. He had gone over to the fountain near the paint booth for a drink and had taken too long to rinse his mouth, and when he came back to the line he found a row of station wagons traveling quite fast, all needing hooks. Aided by Kevin, he worked swiftly and surely, carrying the heavy hooks two at a time; but in his haste he must have overlooked one, for at the head of the line Buster the foreman was waving to him angrily, and the assistant supervisor, his long, equine face pallid with rage under the pale glow of the banked fluorescent lamps, was shouting, "A door hook! A door hook!"

LeRoy ran up the line with the red primer-covered hook in his gloved hand and leaped up the metal steps to the upward-rising line where two metal finishers and a solderer were working frantically under the angry eye of the white-shirted supervisor. Startled by the sudden distraction of the heavy red hook as it flashed past his plexiglass goggles, the solderer raised his right arm for an instant. The flow gun that he held shot a stream of roaring blue-yellow flame directly at LeRoy's mouth.

"Look out!" Kevin cried.

LeRoy jumped back instinctively from the flame, his heavy shoe became entangled with the hose of the metal finisher's buzzing grinder, and he lost his footing. Trying not to drop the heavy cast-iron hook, which might have dented the finished body, he swung his left hand out for support, found none, and fell backwards from the platform at the end of the line which jutted out like a diving board.

Off balance, and with his feet snarled as though bound, LeRoy crashed down against the open-swung door of a station-wagon body like a bound victim presented to the guillotine. Blood spurted from his neck as the air hose snapped with an explosive *bang-hiss!*, the grinding machine stopped, and the disembodied loudspeaker voice crowed senselessly, "Mr. Gaxton, Mr. Gaxton."

Slipping in his own blood as he tried to rise, LeRoy saw three things happen as clearly as though he were sitting in the movies with Lily: the supervisor raced for the phone, Buster ran out to the aisle to stop a passing tricycle, and huge Kevin swayed like an axed tree and fell senseless to the concrete floor.

LeRoy was still conscious, although now the ocean of pain was rising to film over the clarity of the scene, as three of the sweating men, their hands covered with the blood that gushed so from his neck that the slash could not be seen, dragged him across the floor to the big tricycle and placed him carefully on its rear wooden platform. From there he saw Kevin rise dizzily to his knees, and he tried to call farewell to him, but only bubbling noises came from his throat as he was wheeled away.

Lying more alone in the hospital bed than he had ever been in his life, LeRoy said to himself, I don't need anybody to draw me a diagram. He took the doctors' explanations politely but coldly, as if they were only telling him something he had known for a long time, and when Lily came to sit on the white metal chair at his side and to rest her head, black as a bird's wing against the institutional sheet, near his arm, he patted her carefully, in the way he already knew she liked. He raised her face by the chin so he could stare fixedly into her brilliant Indian eyes.

"Indian eyes," he whispered, watching them flood with tears. "Just like your grandmammy's."

"Thank God," she cried, "thank God you're all right. You'll see, everything will work out fine."

He took his hand from her chin and placed it lightly across her mouth.

"We're not kids any more, we're raising a family. You be careful and don't slip on the way home, you hear? We lose one thing, let's not lose another."

In the weeks that followed, LeRoy lay staring at the pinholes in the acoustical tiles of the hospital ceiling and thinking of the assembly line from which he had been trundled away like a bloody infant. The weather was turning warm. It must be getting hot, he imagined, under the factory's stagelike rows of fluorescent lights, where the men performed their daily act of pantomime without his vocal accompaniment. Different men, most likely, since a lot of them had probably already returned thankfully to construction work and to other outdoor jobs. Still, there must be a hard core of steady men; those were the ones, he thought, who must have organized the collection for him and sent him the present, and it must have been one of them who had inserted with the present a note signed *Body Shop Gang, Day Shift:* "Good luck, Caruso! LeRoy, don't sign anything, until you see the union lawyer."

One day he walked back in, put on his freshly laundered coveralls on which the stains were no more visible than the ineradicable red primer, slipped on his heavy cotton gloves, and reported to Buster. He was very conscious, more so than in weeks, of the thick, neatly taped bandage around his neck, startlingly white against the blackness of his skin, like a clerical collar, but he did not touch it.

"How's it going, kid?" asked Buster.

LeRoy nodded wordlessly.

One of the old-timers came up and said, "Welcome back."

And LeRoy replied, "Thanks a lot."

Kevin was most uncomfortable with him. "When you were gone, after a while it did seem all like a dream."

"It's no dream. Here I am."

"I have been keeping thinking that if I hadn't yelled at you, you might never have tripped and fallen."

"Makes no difference. Sometimes when you ride too high you know you're going to fall. Makes no difference who yells."

Kevin laughed nervously. "I fainted, just like a baby."

"I probably would've too."

"How's your wife, LeRoy?"

"Just fine." He did not elaborate. In fact he did not want to talk at all. It seemed to him that everyone, especially Kevin, could hear how husky and coarsened his voice had become, as though he had been smoking too much.

Later in the day he watched some of the men ease up to Kevin, casually, one at a time, all too obviously to ask about him, what he felt like, whether he had gotten compensation yet, whether he intended to stick it out on the job or was he just waiting for the payoff. But he did not encourage Kevin to ask these things of him. He knew his partner could see that the mimeographed sheets were gone from his toolbox, and that he no longer held the little metal dingus cupped in his glove, or even in his coverall pocket.

And everyone saw, and he no longer cared that they saw, that he no longer smiled. He was unfailingly polite to everyone, he did what he was assigned, and he did at least his share. But he had nothing left to say. And he never sang again.

TWO

Fawn, With a Bit of Green

FOR KEVIN, his employment by the automobile factory was like a child's ticket of admission to an awesome, half-believed-in fairyland of new sights, sounds, colors, and odors. Even the preliminary physical examination, which his nude fellow job applicants, shivering in their stockinged feet, swore was just too damned much like the army, was a revelation to Kevin, who had not been in the United States long enough to learn how to conceal his astonishment. The young men in line with him grumbled and cursed, or stood embarrassed at their physical inadequacies; but Kevin — six feet two, sturdy as an oak, white-skinned and freckled from the roots of the flaming hair, standing up and away from his forehead, to the outer edges of his massive shoulders — was more interested in the complexity of the X-ray equipment and impressed by the fact that he was being examined for nothing.

"Think of it now," he remarked to his companions. "If you were to go to a doctor or a hospital and ask to be checked up like this, I have no doubt they'd charge you a small fortune."

The nervous mutterers refrained from laughing at his naïveté, partly because Kevin was so obviously fresh off the boat and partly because he was too big a man to take chances with. When, the examination over, they were led into the factory itself by the personnel man, after a perfunctory indoctrination, Kevin's natural exuberance could really find expression.

"Look at it all, will you?" he cried.

All of his senses were assailed at once in this vast, endless, steel and concrete world. With the others he crossed the final assembly line and its moving ranks of slick and shiny automobiles; veered around mountainous breastworks of stacked tires; filed past unsmiling men upholstering seats with small pliers and quick fingers, spot-welding frames with spitting weapons, pounding on trunk lids with huge mallets, entering paint booths on echoing wooden clogs in hooded coveralls taped closed at wrists and throat like spacemen; and moved fearlessly under the grid of an overhead conveyer line of brilliant chrome grilles and swinging fenders in yellow, blue, green, red, and a tan that looked, Kevin thought, like what he had always conceived the color fawn to be, a soft and lovely pale, pale brown. At last he was dropped off in the body department, shown where to punch the time clock (in itself a miracle, no less — you slipped the card in the slot and the clock automatically registered the time in tenths and hundredths of an hour!), and turned over to his new boss. Buster the foreman put a fresh cigar in his mouth, wrote down Kevin's time-clock number on a sheet mounted on a clipboard, and presented him unceremoniously to a big black man named LeRoy, who needed a partner attaching cast-iron hooks to the moving bodies on the assembly line.

Sent to the tool crib for an apron, hammer, gloves, and toolbox, Kevin got lost. He got lost again on his way back from lunch in the enormous cafeteria, but LeRoy covered up for him so that nobody was the wiser, and he had the chance to see things he might otherwise not have discovered for months, if ever: heaps of glass higher than his head (or was it plastic, curved as perhaps glass could never be?) with one great mass apparently smashed in transit and sown with ominous red tickets; railway tracks with goods wagons right inside the factory, where shouting men unloaded stamped-out sides of automobiles and carefully crated stacks of bright red motors and black shiny inner organs that he could not even identify; trucking platforms too, where giant silver vans were disgorging cast-iron and aluminum parts; and the entire trim department, where the gleaming newborn autos were fitted out with glittering chrome ornamentation and accessories as they filed in stately procession past the seemingly humble and dirty workers.

How on earth could a man find his way around this Arabian Nights, this extravaganza of noise, color, and smell coursing straight off in every direction as far as the eye could see? Kevin was too embarrassed to ask. Later he learned that high on each pillar at every aisle were a number and a letter — if you knew those of your own department, it was easy enough to chart your course among the latitudes and longitudes of this little world.

But it was not too easy to comprehend it. Kevin was gregarious by nature, and quickly became friendly with several of the men on the line besides his partner LeRoy. Kevin was numbed, however, by the sophistication of the men with whom he worked, even of Negroes from Southern farms who, he was sure, had had less schooling than he. He knew that his questions about the wonders of this dreamlike factory must sound silly even to someone as sympathetic as LeRoy — "How on earth do they ever get the toilets to flush, with the lavatory up there hanging from the ceiling and only a flight of steps tying it to the ground?" or "Do you realize that all these flaming flow guns look like the torches of medieval castles in the cinema?" or "What makes everything come together at the end so that the yellow fenders swing down to meet the yellow cars?" — and, feeling the fool, kept his thoughts more to himself.

Even the people in his rooming house and in the Irish neighborhood where he lived were phlegmatic. Stout O'Bannon, owner of the Shamrock House, yawned in his face when Kevin attempted to convey to him what it was like to be part of an operation in which three hundred automobiles were manufactured every day. Men of substance, grave-faced Farrell the undertaker and lynxlike Flaherty of the Emerald Tourist Service just next door, were frank in telling him that they had dropped in to O'Bannon's for a brew and a few innings of the ball game, not for Kevin's impressions of a scene which was — if not actually unpleasant and lower-class — both familiar and boring.

So Kevin set himself to tell his elderly parents and his spinster sister in his letters why it was that he felt he had found America, the vastness and variety and magic efficiency of it, in the factory. But he was not a natural writer, and it was agonizing for him to attempt lengthy descriptions in letters intended primarily for assurances that all went well with him, that he was saving money and seeing the sights. Besides, after a day's labor it was hard to sit alone in his little room with no company but a ball-point pen and a sheet of blank stationery that had to be filled, when he could have been playing skee-ball or watching TV at the Shamrock House, or dancing with Peggy, who worked at the lunchroom across the way from Farrell's Mortuary Parlor.

Being a sensible man, Kevin compromised. From time to time he wrote the family brief descriptions, he romanced with Peggy and bantered with the neighborhood people, and he went on working hard for his weekly pay check. But since he was a romantic too, Kevin was secretly convinced that somehow he was working for more than that. For he retained somewhere deep within himself an untainted core of wonder and pride, and he knew that one day it would find expression.

What troubled him and nearly shook his faith was that his fellow workers were not merely indifferent, they were actively hostile to their surroundings and to what they did with their own hands. Their talk was continually seasoned with contemptuous references to the factory, to their work, and to the lives they led. Almost everybody who discussed it with him hated the work and admitted frankly that the only incentive to return from one day to the next was the pay check; always they spoke of leaving for something better, something easier and more pleasant, and often they did leave, so that just as a man was becoming friendly and willing to explain why he too cried, "What a way to make a living!" he would show up with a white shirt and tie and a broad grin, pick up his toolbox, announce that he had quit, and disappear from your life forever.

The best of the men and often the most pleasant were those who like Kevin's partner LeRoy had other interests. For them the factory was a necessary evil, a pill that had to be swallowed in order that they could go ahead with what really mattered. Invariably their question was, "What did you do before you came here?" and to Kevin at least it implied a corollary: "What are you going to do when you get out of here?"

He could hardly explain to someone like LeRoy, who lived only for his music and his dream of becoming an opera singer, that just getting out of his village and coming to America and getting a job in this factory bigger than his entire home town was enough in itself. For LeRoy the assembly plant was nothing, literally nothing, to come to; it was just something to endure, as his ancestors had probably endured slavery while dreaming of a better state. So the partners discussed music when they could, which was a great boon to LeRoy, who leaned toward Kevin's understanding as a plant inclines toward the sun.

Then LeRoy slipped on the line, gashing his throat as he fell, and Kevin, seeing the blood gush forth from his friend's slashed neck, fell to the floor himself in a red haze of shock and horror.

Unlike many of the men around him, Kevin had fought in no wars and was utterly unused to living with blood or ideas of violence. During the weeks of LeRoy's recuperation Kevin too had to recuperate from the shame of having fainted, even though everyone considerately avoided discussing his collapse. It was for him a period of revaluation. He began to feel that he too should have, like LeRoy and the men he most admired, an ambition going beyond what he had already achieved.

As soon as he had put it to himself that bluntly, he knew what it was that he wanted. He started to live more frugally, to pinch down his living expenses and to exist almost as meanly as a miser, banking the greater part of his pay; and then he looked around him, almost as calculatingly, for someone to confide in, someone to confirm his tentative and daring decision.

At last he determined to speak to young Walter. In a way, it was Walter who sought him out, for this snub-nosed eighteen-year-old with the ready smile and the head of crew-cut blond hair was amused and captivated by Kevin's Irish accent; and although there were ten hard years between them, they soon became mutual confidants.

Wiping the sweat from his forehead (he was being broken in as a metal finisher and found the filing terribly hard), Walter took advantage of a line stoppage to ask, "Say, where do you come from, anyway?"

"County Kerry. You probably never heard of it, no big cities or the like of that for you to learn of it."

"What'd you do there?" Walter too had to ask the standard question, the opening query in the eternal attempt to find a community of interest.

Kevin said bluntly, for as yet he was unaware of the gulf his answer might have opened up with another man, "I was a schoolmaster."

"A schoolmaster! In a big school?"

"Oh no," Kevin laughed. "Just myself and a young lady and a one-room country school. Between us we handled seventy or eighty children in all the grades."

"How come you gave it up?"

"The dullness of it," Kevin replied, removing his rusty glove and running his fingers through his thatch of orange hair, "and the heavy hand of the clergy. You don't know the half of it — you can't even get the job without a letter from your parish priest. And after that, it's the religious instruction and education over everything. Seven years of it I had, and decided to see a bit of the world before settling down to the married state."

"Do you like it here?" Walter's tone had the elaborate casualness of a young mother asking for an opinion of her baby's looks.

"Ah, it's fascinatin'!"

"It must be, for you." Then Walter added, as though this was what he had really been itching to say from the beginning: "I'm saving up to be a civil engineer."

"An engineer. Now think of it!"

"I'm trying to put away fifty bucks a week. It's not impossible. I live with my folks. When I have fifteen hundred dollars, I'm going to the state university engineering school."

Kevin was amazed yet again by the richness of the American possibility. "And how long is it that you've been out of high school?"

"Just since last June."

Kevin wanted to ask more, but the line was moving once again, and Walter, the sweat springing from his short-cropped hair as he pushed his file back and forth against the dull steel auto bodies, was far too busy even to look up at Kevin. Walter took the job hard, struggling to do his work well and at the same time keep up with the line and the other metal finishers; and Kevin, the sedentary schoolmaster, who could sling a hundredweight of potatoes over his massive shoulders without straining his back, was moved to pity for the slighter boy and wished that there were only some way to lighten his burden. Mixed with the pity was respect for the dogged ambition of this seemingly happy-go-lucky young American. Kevin came to the conclusion that such a boy was sensible enough, with all his youth, to give a man a straight answer, and when they met during lunch hour in the cafeteria they at once began to talk about what Kevin wanted to know.

"It's a funny thing the way two different people like us should meet in a place like this, isn't it?" mused Walter, gripping his wax-paper-covered sandwich with both half-dried hands and biting into it.

"We're the pawns of fate," sighed Kevin. "That I do believe. We're tossed about from here to there."

"In that case, we should have been tossed to some place better than this."

"There I don't agree with you. For me there is a beauty about it all that I'm finding it very hard to explain to anyone. Just look out there at those elegant shiny cars — a heap of metal parts when they come in here, and lovely limousines when they're driven off the final line. Splendid glittering vehicles even more fine than the way they show up in the magazines. I've been sayin' to myself, what would be more logical than for a man who works here to own one himself?"

"Why not? Lots of them do."

"Yes, but . . ." Kevin hesitated. "I see all the hundreds of cars in the parking lot, and it's a sure bet that they belong to those who have put away a good bit."

"I guess you never heard of financing. Nine out of ten people nowadays can't afford to pay cash. All you need is a trade-in, or a down payment."

"And after you've made this down payment" — Kevin leaned forward so eagerly across the cafeteria table that he upended the two half-pint milk cartons he had just finished, — "is the machine really yours to keep as long as you go on paying every month? Legally yours?"

"Once you make that down payment and they turn over the papers and the car, it's as much yours as anything else you own in this world."

Kevin stared at Walter without seeing him. The vision of himself riding on that cushiony, rubber-stuffed seat, his hands playing easily with the spidery black steering wheel, was so real that he could almost hear the imperious warning of the horn as he pressed the button to clear the road. Then his eyes refocused and he saw Walter looking anxiously at him.

"What's the matter?" Walter asked. "You look like you're going off the deep end."

"Listen," Kevin said tensely. "You're an intelligent lad. Do you think it a foolish ambition for a man like me, a foreigner so to speak, to want to buy a new car?"

"You've got as much right as anybody," Walter replied warmly. "What the hell, you make them. Besides, all you have to do is show a dealer your badge and he has to sell you a car for his price plus ten per cent. You'll save quite a few hundred dollars that way."

Kevin felt his heart thumping painfully in his chest. "But you don't think it silly or extravagant of me? Every day I hear the men making fun of the cars, saying how terrible they are, how cheaply made, how overpriced."

"But people always talk like that where they work, unless they own the place. You don't see any of them walking to work, do you? And what's more, most of them buy the same car they help to build. Why not? No, don't pay any attention to that kind of talk. Nobody's going to laugh at you for buying one."

"You see," Kevin said tentatively, "it might seem a bit peculiar to you, but I'll be the first one in my family ever to own an auto. It'd be a bit of a thrill for the folks to get a snap of me sitting at the wheel of my smart new car. People just don't have the money back home that they do here. Ireland's organized differently, and then, it's a poor country."

"Of course," Walter replied. "I understand."

They arose to return to the line, stacking their refuse on a moving conveyer at the exit door as they left the cafeteria.

"Got any particular model in mind?" Walter asked.

Kevin laughed shyly. "Oh, I haven't thought that far yet. But I have been thinking somewhat about the color. They say you can practically choose the colors you want in the two-tone models. Is that right?"

"Within reason."

"Well, that I *have* been dreaming of, you might say. I thought when the time came I'd order it in fawn, with a bit of green. That doesn't sound outrageous or unreasonable, does it?"

Walter pursed his lips. "No, I don't think so. I'm trying to visualize it."

"The green, well, that would be for the old Irish, you know. And the fawn would be just for me, because I like it."

Walter did not laugh, merely nodded as they moved hurriedly down the aisle into the howling of the siren that announced the end of the lunch hour; and Kevin, grateful for the young boy's understanding, was now confirmed in the belief that he had embarked on the right road for himself. That night he enrolled in a driving school.

Whereas before his feet had ached at the end of a long day on the concrete floor, now they were springy and willing to carry him to work without complaining; whereas before even he, the thrilled alien, had confessed to a certain weariness with the monotony of his repeated task, now he marveled at the speed with which the hours, yes, and the days flew by, as pay check followed pay check and his life flowed onwards irresistibly towards his goal like a great sluggish river seeking the sea.

Even the factory itself, to which he had been growing insensibly accustomed, became renewed in wonder as he recognized about him the parts that would be fashioned into his own automobile: the racks of radios, cushion fabrics, and ventilator ducts, ablaze with color and wheeled towards their ultimate destination like troops deployed into battle areas, were more important to him than the men with whom he worked, for the men were merely ignorant, profane laborers, exhausting themselves without knowing why, while the immaculate inner organs of the automobiles, smelling faintly of preserving oil and newness, seemed to announce by their very profusion and *hardness* that they were inexhaustible. Kevin watched the drops of nacreous sweat forming on Walter's forehead as the boy pushed furiously with his file at the resistant steel, and was unmoved; he greeted his former partner LeRoy when the big black man came back after his accident, but had little to say to him now that their separate ambitions had taken such opposite courses, one already disastrously foundered, the other well on its way toward fulfillment.

At last Kevin was able to walk into the automobile dealer's, as easily as Walter had predicted. He placed his order with a snappy red-faced compatriot who assured him that he was going to get a special break because he came from County Kerry.

"I've decided on the convertible hard-top," Kevin murmured, one leg dangling from the showroom automobile as casually as though this was something he did every year.

"Good to find a man who knows his mind," applauded the salesman. "You don't know what we go through with wives sometimes. And for color?"

Kevin was on the point of replying spontaneously, "Fawn, with a bit of green, is what I've had in mind from the very first," but something almost like shame stopped him. Instead he said with false judiciousness, "I'd like a tan, a pale brown, with green for the second color."

The salesman laughed ingratiatingly. "Wouldn't do to leave out the old shamrock, would it? But that's a special order job — you may have to wait a while for those colors."

Kevin nodded. "I can wait."

It was on a Saturday morning that the dealer notified him-that his car was ready. Kevin stopped in at a drugstore on the way and bought a roll of color film for the camera with which Peggy had promised to come out from the lunchroom and take his picture. When the dealer handed him the keys in a little leatherette case and waved him away from the curb so that he merged with the traffic and became one with its aimless but rapid flow, Kevin, his heart hammering, felt that at last he had become an American.

Waiting for him in front of his rooming house were not only faithful Peggy and her expensive camera, but Farrell the undertaker and Flaherty the travel agent and a bunch of the regulars from the Shamrock House. Kevin took it like a man, accepting the handshakes and congratulations coolly and posing calmly both behind the wheel and standing at the side of his automobile.

"That one'll give the old folks a thrill!" someone called out.

"That's what it's for," Kevin replied nonchalantly.

As soon as he decently could, Kevin separated himself from the tire-kickers and dashboard-inspectors and drove off alone, waving a breezy farewell as though it were nothing for him to drive with one hand. It took him an hour to grope his way out of the city, until he could drive at ease through the burgeoning countryside, singing aloud in rough tune to the dance music of his push-button radio. When he returned later in the day, he was just a little surprised to find that there was no one waiting for him this time, only a couple of youngsters playing leapfrog over the fire hydrant, and even they barely looked up when he brought the car to the curb.

That night he took Peggy for a ride. It was considerably more classy than walking to a dance hall or standing in line at the Majestic waiting for the last show. Unquestionably it put Peggy in the mood for romancing, when he tuned in soft music and wrapped his right arm about her; but she took no other interest in the car at all beyond its existence as proof that Kevin was rising in the world.

So the next day, which was Sunday, Kevin went to Mass for his parents' sake and got into the car alone, after having wiped and dusted it. He drove about the city all morning and then tried out the country again in the afternoon, keeping well within the speed limit advised for breaking in. But the sky turned gray as metal filings over the hills at the horizon, and by the time he got back it was raining hard. He made sure the windows were rolled tight and dashed into the hallway, leaving the car parked at the curb. Once in his room, he wiped his head with a towel and parted the curtains behind the dresser to look down at his car three

stories below. All that he could see by the vague glow of
the just-lighted street lamp was the rain beating steadily on
its roof and hood, hammering like nails against the metal;
he could no longer make out the colors.

At five-thirty in the morning Kevin climbed into the car
in his work clothes, arranging a moth-eaten Indian blanket
under him so that he would not soil the plastic seat covers,
and made his way carefully through the dirty industrial
dawn to the automobile factory. He parked the car in the
immense lot and hastened inside without a backward glance,
for the ride had taken longer than he had anticipated.

The line was already moving by the time he had put on
his apron and gloves. He set to work at once, with hardly a
moment for a nod to his boss or the metal finishers around
him. Within an hour he found himself trying to calculate
the time remaining before his twelve-minute break; he
looked up, bored and annoyed with himself, into the bleak,
accusing eyes of LeRoy, who still wore a narrow taped
bandage around his throat, not, Kevin was sure, because
he needed it any longer, but because he was still embarrassed by the wound. LeRoy shrugged his neck down into
his coveralls and turned away. Confused, Kevin too swung
about and found himself gazing into the sweat-rimmed eyes
of young Walter, straightening up with a desperate groan
from a dent he had been hopelessly trying to knock out and
file down. The boy's face, smudged across the cheekbones
and under the eyes from where he had wiped off running
perspiration with the back of his oily glove, looked, falsely

— and yet not so falsely — as though he had been crying.

What *is* this? Kevin asked himself suddenly. Is this the excitement and the adventure that I sought? He bumped his kneecap painfully against a steel dolly and to his astonishment felt a stream of foul words, meaningless factory curses that he would never have dreamed of using back home, rushing up into his throat as palpably as vomit. As soon as he had uttered them, he experienced a feeling of release so startling that he stopped work, shocked into immobility. Now that he had learned how to swear like the others, learned what it meant to have something to curse at, maybe *now* he was a proper American at last.

For he had gained what he so dearly wanted, and he saw with bitter clarity that he would be chained to the line for years, chained to the drudgery, the monotony, the grinding labor — all of which lost their novelty and certainly their glamor when you had won your prize — literally until the prize itself had become valueless and demanded that you replace it with another, shinier one.

The day was the longest he had ever worked. Even after lunch the hours dragged interminably; by the time he had punched out and gotten his windbreaker from his locker, his feet, rested from the week end's driving, were swollen and burning. But he walked as fast as he could to the lot, where his automobile was waiting with those of all his fellow workers to carry him swiftly away from the factory.

In the middle of the lot he paused, looked around, and then realized that he could not remember where he had parked his car. There were ten rows, each row with nearly a hundred automobiles toed up to the white stripe, and in the smoky light of the waning afternoon it was very hard to tell them apart. Almost all were the same make, almost all were recent models, and all were streaked and spotted with the drying remnants of the day's rain. When at last he found his own car, in the middle of a long line that he had already circled twice, each time with increasing weariness and contempt for his own stupidity, Kevin saw that it too was not merely speckled with dirt, but was caked with dried mud at the wheels and hubcaps. And was it possible, was there already a spot òf rust on the front bumper? There was something there, the color and texture of dried blood. Kevin could not bring himself to bend down and look.

He squeezed in stiffly behind the wheel and drove off slowly, thinking for the first time in many days of LeRoy's terrible accident and of the blood that had spurted from his neck onto the steel body of the passing car as he fell. He shuddered, and as he did so he remembered how LeRoy, no longer singing, had turned sadly away from him and how desperately Walter had looked up at him this very morning with the droplets of sweat clinging to his eyebrows and dripping onto the metal that he filed. Kevin had gotten the colors he wanted for his automobile, but now it bore other stigmata that he had never envisioned.

When he arrived at his rooming house, Kevin asked his landlady for a piece of cardboard. On it he lettered with schoolteacherly neatness:

4 SALE. ENQUIRE AT
EMERALD TOURIST SERVICE

He propped up the finished sign against his windshield, locked the car, and with the keys in his fist crossed the sidewalk to the tourist agency, where crafty-faced Flaherty, the light above his desk already turned on against the dying day, was filling out a tax return. Kevin tapped lightly on the counter top with his ignition key. Flaherty glanced up, annoyed, and nodded curtly.

"I'm here on business."

Flaherty arose and came forward to face him. "And what's the business?"

"Could you be telling me the price of a ticket to Cobh?"

Automatically, Flaherty reached for his schedule sheets, wet his thumb with the tip of his tongue, and began to shuffle the papers. Suddenly he paused and glanced sharply, shrewdly, at Kevin. "Round trip, is it, or just one way?"

"One way."

Flaherty's eyebrows went up. "You haven't had bad news from home?"

"No, there's no special news from home. There seldom is. It's a dull and stagnant place, my town." Kevin looked at him steadily. "It's me that'll be bringing them the news." And he opened his hand and let the keys fall lightly to the counter.

THREE

Joe, the Vanishing American

IF WALTER had not been so desperately anxious to go away to college, he might never have been able to stick it out those first few weeks at the factory. His father, once district sales manager for a bankrupted sewing-machine concern, had come down in the world and was now a continually uneasy clerk in the branch office of a usury outfit called the Friendly Finance Corporation; his mother, who had borne Walter late in life, clung jealously to the fading prestige conferred on her by her many beneficences on behalf of the Ladies' Guild.

Walter had never done anything harder than shovel the neighbors' snowy driveways and sell magazines to reluctant relatives. But the night of his graduation from high school his father grunted in a choked voice that there was no money to send him to college. Walter swore to himself that he would get a college education if he had to rob a bank. At the commencement exercises a classmate had told him that you could get a job at the new auto assembly plant if you said on your application that you had worked as a garage mechanic. While his parents rocked creakily, proud but miserable, on the porch glider, Walter mounted the narrow steps to his little room and sat down at his desk. If he could work steadily at the plant for a year he ought to be able to save several thousand dollars even after contributing his share of the household expenses. Without saying a word to his parents, he went to the plant the following morning and filled out an application blank. Three days later he received a telegram asking him to report for work at six-thirty A.M.

When he returned, gray and exhausted, from his first long day in the body shop to which he had been assigned, Walter found his mother sitting in the parlor and sobbing into a handkerchief. She raised her eyes at the slamming of the door and stared at him in horror.

"Look at you!" she cried, and immediately Walter knew that her first shock was at the way he *looked*, not at how he must have *felt*. Nevertheless Walter felt it his filial duty to explain that he would not have to march past the neighbors in greasy coveralls, but could wear sport clothes to work and change at the plant; furthermore, he hinted, when his mother was preparing his sandwiches for the next day's lunch, he could just as easily carry them in a little paper bag as in a metal lunch box.

His father, keeping them company in the kitchen, took a different tack, and even blustered a little about the advantages of working for a huge corporation.

"I don't see why Walter couldn't have started with something more pleasant," his mother said plaintively, smoothing mayonnaise across white bread. "In an office he could at least use his brains."

"Don't kid yourself," her husband replied. "There's no shame attached to factory work any more. Besides, Walter has a darned good chance to advance if he shows them the stuff he's got."

Implicit in all this was his parents' fear that Walter had started down a dead-end street, and their own shame at not having been able to send him away to college. Anxious not to inflame their feelings, Walter refrained from defending his decision; even if he were only to point out that he would be making big money, it would be a direct insult to his father, who at fifty-nine was making only five dollars a week more than he. So he put the case negatively.

"There's just no place else around," he said, "that would pay me anything like what I'm going to be making at the auto plant."

"The boy is right, Mother," his father said decisively, much to Walter's satisfaction. "You're doing a smart thing, Walter."

Thus challenged at home, Walter had no alternative but to grit his teeth and swear to himself that nothing would make him quit until he had reached his goal. Like a groggy but game boxer, he measured out his future not with the end of the fight in view, for that would have been too far away, but rather in terms of more immediate accomplishments: his first automatic nickel raise at the end of four weeks, his second automatic nickel raise at the end of eight weeks, his acceptance as a permanent employee at the end of ninety days, and most of all his listing as a metal finisher, which would mean that he would be in the highest-paid group in the plant and that he would be recognized as a skilled worker, a man who had made the grade.

His surroundings meant nothing to Walter, who had not expected that the factory would look like an art gallery. But the work, and the conditions under which he had to do it, were a nightmare of endless horror from which Walter sometimes thought, stumbling wearily out of the plant after ten hours of unremitting anguish, he would one day awaken with a scream. It was not simply that the idea of working on an endless succession of auto bodies as they came slowly but ineluctably rolling down the asembly line like so many faceless steel robots was both monotonous and stupefying, or that the heavy work of finding bumps and dents in them, knocking them out and filing them down, was in itself too exhausting.

No, it was the strain of having to work both fast and accurately, with the foreman standing over him and glaring through his thick-lensed glasses, that made Walter dread the beginning of each day. Under the best of conditions, he figured, he had three and a half minutes to complete his

metal-finishing work from the time he started a job on his
line to the time it reached the platform and was swung off
on hooks toward the bonderizing booth. If he began at the
very beginning, as soon as the inspector had indicated bad
spots with a stump of chalk, circling hollows and X-ing high
spots, he could finish before the job reached the final inspector at the far end of the line — unless the dents were
too deep or too numerous, in which case he was still madly
pounding and filing, squatting and straining with the sweat
running down his temples and his cheekbones while the
solder flower worked next to him in a tangle of rubber hose,
melting lead, and a blazing gun with a flame so hot that it
scorched dry the running sweat on his face, and the final
inspector stood over him, imperturbably chalking newly
discovered hollows and pimples in the infuriating metal.
Then he would straighten up from his hopeless effort and
with a despairing glance at the impassive pick-up man, who
had to finish what he had left undone, he would hurry back
down the line, praying to dear God that the next car — he
did every third one — would be in fairly decent condition.

Worst of all were the times when he would hear a pierc-
ing whistle and would look up from the damnable dent at
which he had been rapping blindly with the point of his
file to see Buster the foreman all the way past the platform,
waving at him angrily with his cigar. Hurrying from his
unfinished work to his punishment, Walter would try to
steel himself against what he knew was coming, but it was
no use.

"You call yourself a metal man?" Buster would ask, stuffing the cigar between his teeth with an angry snap. "You want to get metal finisher's pay and you let a job like that go through?" His eyes glinting with rage behind his thick spectacles, Buster would gesticulate at one of Walter's cars, freshly speckled with chalk marks as it swung in the air. "Get going on it!"

And Walter would hurl himself at the job, dashing the sweat from his brow with the back of his gloved hand and filing away in a clumsy fury.

By the time he had somehow or other repaired what he had left undone, he would find on hastening back to the line that he was far behind once again in his regular work, so far behind that it might take him the better part of an hour to gradually work his way back on the line to where he really belonged, safe for the moment from shouted complaints.

Inevitably the men around him had suggestions as to how Walter might better his condition. Of the two other metal finishers who worked on the line with him, one was a dour, fattish man, a leader in the opposition of the local union and disgusted because it did nothing to provide security for probationary employees like Walter.

"I'll tell you something else. There's countries where a bright young hard-working fellow like you, that wants to go to college, doesn't have to waste the best years of his life in factory work just to save the money for college fees. He gets sent right through school and the government foots the bills. All he has to do is show that he's got the stuff and his future is secure."

Walter allowed that this sounded fine, although "having the stuff" sounded uncomfortably like his father's eulogies of life in America, but he could not see what practical good it did him here and now — unless he was supposed to get satisfaction from the bitterness of knowing that in mysterious other countries his opposite numbers were better off than he.

The third metal finisher, a lean, efficient, sardonic man, had been listening silently to this talk of free college careers. He put his wiry hand inside his open-necked khaki shirt, scratched the coarse curling hair below his throat, and laughed aloud.

"What's the matter?" asked his fattish colleague suspiciously.

"You think your propaganda's going to change this boy's ideas about the other side of the world, when everything here tells him he's got it so good?" He tapped the fat man on the shoulder with the butt end of his file as patronizingly as if he were patting him on the head. "Even if he has to suffer for his education in a way that shouldn't be necessary, he's free. He can blunder around and maybe even learn something that isn't listed in the college catalogues. Those poor kids you want him to envy, they may be getting their college for nothing, but they're paying a higher price for it than this fellow ever will. And the sad part is that most of them probably don't even know what the price is."

And he turned back to his work without giving the fat man a chance to reply.

Fortunately for the three of them, the fat metal finisher was transferred. He was only replaced, however, by an intense worker with two vertical wrinkles between his brows, who watched Walter's ineffectual work with growing impatience. At last he could stand it no more.

"In this game, kid, the knack of it is in the speed. The speed," he said fiercely, "and the way you concentrate on the job. If you're going to fumble around and just bitch about your mistakes, you'll be a long time getting straightened out." He greeted his own badly dented job, rolling towards them, with a smile of genuine pleasure. "Size it up quick, pick out the worst dents, and get going on them right away. Leave the high spots for last — the pick-up men don't mind doing them."

The third man, the gray-haired cynic whom everyone liked but no one seemed to know, had been listening quietly, with a strange, mild grin on his long and youthful face. He put a stick of chewing gum in his mouth, ruminated for a moment, and said: "What you really want is for him to enjoy his work, Orrin. Might be more practical if you'd get down and actually show him how to do it. Here, hold on a minute, Walter."

Walter had been squatting on his haunches before the wheel housing of his job, blindly pounding with a hammer at his hidden screwdriver, trying hopelessly to punch a hole underneath so that with the screwdriver he could dig out a deep dent as the others did, trying so hopelessly that as he smashed the hammer against his left hand, missing the butt end of the screwdriver, he had to squeeze his eyes to keep the tears from starting forth.

"Give me that screwdriver."

Handing up the tool to the laconic man, Walter noticed for the first time that he bore an unusual tattoo, faded like an old flag, on his right forearm: an American eagle, claws gripping his wrist, beak opened triumphantly at the elbow — you could almost hear it screaming. Without a word the man took the screwdriver and swiftly pressed it to a grinding wheel, fashioning a beveled point.

"Try it now."

Walter stuck the screwdriver under the car, rapped at it smartly several times — *bang!* it was through and resting against the outer skin of the car, just at the very dent. Gratefully, he turned to the gray-haired man, but the man was gone, like a mirage.

There was something miragelike about him, anyway. He drove to and from work alone, he never engaged in small talk, he never hung around with a group at lunch hour or before work, he kept a paper book in the hip pocket of his khaki trousers, and always when he was not concentrating on his own work, when he was watching Walter or listening to the others handing him advice, he had that mocking irreligious smile on his long narrow youthful face. What was more, his cold blue eye seemed always to be on Walter, sizing him up, watching not so much his work, as everyone else did, but his temperament and his personality. It made him uncomfortable.

Gradually Walter began to sort out the other men around him, the ones who had more common reality in their talk and their tastes. Most companionable of them all was Kevin, the former rural schoolteacher, now an immigrant hook man. His accent was so delightful, his turns of speech so happy, that Walter engaged the towering redhead in conversation at every opportunity.

"Hey, Kevin," he shouted at him one day, "how old were those kids you taught in County Kerry?"

"Ah, Walter," Kevin sighed, showing his long white teeth as he spoke, "they weren't *all* such children. If you were to see some of the older girls — quite well-developed, they were. Oh, how shameful if they had known what was passing through their schoolmaster's mind!"

Kevin laughed at the memory, Walter at the picture the big fellow conjured up of countryside lust; he turned around and there was the gray-haired metal finisher, smiling too, but so coldly you would have thought him a scientist observing a successful experiment. It was chilling, and yet not wholly unpleasant. In a way that he could not define, Walter felt that he was being judged and approved.

This third man, reserved and anonymous as ever, continued to observe him as Walter chatted not only with Kevin and the second metal finisher but with all of the other men on their line. Conversation was necessarily shouted and fragmentary, but Walter was astonished at how intimacies could be revealed in the course of a few phrases:

"A man's a fool to get married."

"Grab the overtime while you can. In the auto industry you never know when you'll be laid off."

"Happiest time of my life was when I was in the army."

"Only reason I'm here is because I was too stupid to learn a trade."

"I came here out of curiosity, but my curiosity's all used up."

"My wife says if I quit I'll have a better chance to line up a construction job."

"Walter, don't turn out like those college men who can tell you how to do everything but can't do a damn thing themselves."

The only one to rebuff Walter's friendly overtures was Pop, the seamy-faced little inspector with a rooster's ruff of yellowing white hair that rose and tumbled down over his forehead, and sunken old lips from which depended miraculously a heavy, unlighted cigar. Wizened, pale, and bloodless, he regarded Walter, for no apparent reason, with bottomless contempt. With a little cap perched sideways on his Niagara of a head like a precarious canoe, and a soft brown cloth knotted about the hand with which he probed Walter's work for defects and omissions, he seemed to Walter like some strange and hateful gnome.

"Kids like you," he said in a dry and rusty monotone,

"they come and go. Twenty-three years I'm here, and I seen a million like you. Not steady, not reliable, don't want to learn, just out for fun. You'll never make a metal man."

I don't want to be a metal man, Walter wanted to reply; I just want to make my money and get out of here. But this was, he knew, just what Pop was goading him to say, so he held his tongue. A moment later he was glad that he had, for he was startled to hear the third metal finisher address him.

"Pop is an exception," he said, bending over Walter's car and scrubbing at it with his sandpaper as he spoke. "By and large there is a democracy of age in the factory. Men who have been here since before you were born fought for a union contract guaranteeing equal treatment for you. Ninety days after you start you get the same wage as a worker who's been on the job nineteen years. A man twice your age will treat you as a working partner and an adult. Where else is that true?"

"Yes," Walter replied angrily, "but Pop —"

"He's got reason to be bitter. Someday I'll tell you why."

He straightened up abruptly and walked away to his own job. But the words he had used reverberated in Walter's mind. Who was he, with his young-old face and his expressions like "democracy of age"? Walter asked, but no one seemed to know. Some said he was a seaman and adventurer, and his big tattoo was pointed to as proof, for he had been heard to state himself that he had acquired it in Lourenço Marques; but others, who had themselves come to the assembly line from rural homesteads, were positive from clues he had let fall that he had formerly been an itinerant farm laborer; and there were even those who swore that he was really an educated man, a kind of college professor amusing himself by slumming among them.

Whoever he was, for the time he had nothing more to say. But Walter felt his presence, for he was always ready to lend a hand, always laconically helpful, always silently observing and listening.

One day the younger inspector at the beginning of the line, blowing genial clouds of illegal pipe smoke, gave Walter some frank and cynical advice.

"Been listening to the bosses talking about you, buddy." He took the pipe from his mouth and formed a fat smoke ring. "Want to know what's wrong with what you're doing?"

"I guess so," said Walter dully.

"You try too hard. You're trying to do a good job — that's the worst thing you can do."

Walter stared in bewilderment at the inspector. "But why?"

"They're interested in pulling production. If you're going to be running up and down the line all day trying to make every job perfect, you're just going to get in people's way. What the bosses will do is, they'll look for an excuse to fire you before your probationary period is up, or else they'll stick you in a routine lower-paying job."

"Then . . ."

"I've been here ten years. Believe me" — he drew on his pipe once again and smiled disarmingly — "they're not interested in making good cars, they're interested in making cars. You know what production means? Volume. And you know what they hired you for? To camouflage, not to get rid of every flaw. Hide them so they don't show up after the car's been through paint, so the customer doesn't see them at the dealer's, and you'll get along great."

"Camouflage them how?"

"With your sandpaper. With the grinding wheel. If you hit them up and down and then across, final inspection will never know what's underneath. Make it look good, and confusing. Be a camouflage artist and the bosses'll very seldom bother you."

Walter could not help laughing. "Listen, how could you stand it here for ten years? Every day I think maybe I ought to get out and look for something else."

"For six years," the inspector said pleasantly, "I was like you. This was going to be just temporary until I found something with a real future. It took me six years to realize that I was going to be spending the rest of my life here — it's like breaking in a wild horse, only with a human being it takes longer. I got married, had three kids, now I'm building a home near the plant. So I make the best of it, I take it easy and I have as much fun as I can, and I hate to see a guy like you breaking his back all for nothing."

Bending over his work, Walter raised his file and heard the inspector's final shot, lightly enough intended but bearing its own weight of bitterness and resignation: "You'd be surprised how many fellows I've heard talking just like you — couldn't stand the work, going to quit any day — and now they're five- and ten-year men, starting to think about retirement benefits."

Walter could not clarify in his own mind what it was about the inspector's attitude that increased his desperation, not until his silent partner eased up to him from nowhere and said quietly, "Kind of terrified you, didn't he?"

"Not exactly terrified."

"Just the same, it's no fun to be doing time and to be told that your sentence just might turn out to be indefinite. Then if you've got a good imagination you can see yourself gradually getting used to it, even getting to like the routine, so that one day follows another and the first thing you know the wrinkles are there and the kids are grown up and you don't know where it's all gone to, your life."

Walter felt himself shuddering. Was it from the blower overhead that he felt his hot sweat turning cold and drying on his face? He said, "I suppose you have to be cynical if you're going to stay here."

"Day after day your life becomes a joke without any point, a trick that you play on yourself from punching in to punching out."

"But that's only if you're an imaginative or a sensitive person."

For the first time, the man's angular face hardened. "Don't you think somebody like that inspector had his ambitions? Don't you think he still has his man's pride? Did you ever figure the cost of the job in terms of what it does to the personality of a clever, intelligent fellow like him? He says if you're going to be trapped you might as well make the best of it, and by his lights he may be right. Anyway don't be too quick to blame him — he probably never had the opportunity to save money and go off to college."

No one had ever, not ever in eighteen years, talked to Walter in such a way. He would never again be able to look at a man like the inspector without compassion. Even at home in the evening with his father, whom he could no longer talk to about anything but baseball or the weather (although they both tried clumsily to broach other more serious topics), Walter found that he was viewing this desolate man not just as his father but as a man who had his own miseries; and this, he knew, was a part of growing up that could not have come about as it had without the influence of his strange friend in the factory.

More and more as the weeks passed and exhaustion was gradually overcome by vitality, only to be transformed into monotony, Walter came to feel that only this man could explain the real meaning of the assembly line. But he remained aloof, insubstantial as a ghost. The more he held to himself, the more Walter was piqued, and determined to make the ghost speak.

At last one day he ventured to demand: "Say, what does that tattoo of yours stand for, that big bird?"

The man smiled with one side of his mouth. "That old bird is the American eagle." He raised his arm briefly, flexed it, and let it fall to his side. "It's screaming with rage at what's happened to the republic."

"What *has* happened?"

"Where are the guts? Where's the drive? In a place like this a man's life goes down the drain like scummy water."

"But you're working here too," Walter said boldly.

The man shook his head slowly, with such finality that there was something elemental about the gesture. "I'm not a settled-down man. I'm just passing through."

Walter cleared his throat. "I don't even know your name."

"Why should you? Instead of learning names, we refer to the fellow with the bad teeth, or the guy with the blue coveralls. When I work next to a man for months and learn that his wife is being operated on for cancer of the breast and still don't know his name, it tells me something, not just about him and me, but about the half-connections that are all the factory allows you in the way of friendships."

"The old-timers arc clubby enough, but everybody else claims they're here for a limited time. The place is so big and everything seems so temporary that I suppose we don't feel the need of introducing ourselves."

The older man looked at Walter somberly. "No one who comes here wants to admit that the place has any real connection with his real life. He has to say that he is just putting in his time here, and so no matter how friendly he is by nature he has to think of the people around him as essentially strangers, men whom he can't even trouble to say good-by to when he quits or gets laid off."

"But *your* name —"

"Call me Joe."

Walter pursued him: "Every third guy on the line must be named Joe. Joe what?"

He smiled again, his long Yankee countenance creasing in a cold grin. "Joe, the vanishing American." And he turned his back on Walter and bent to his work as the line resumed its endless progress.

But he was a curious man, a nosy man, and he was there, listening and leering, when Walter found a minute to respond without cursing to a bitter remark of Pop's. Walter turned on him with the anger he had managed to suppress when speaking to the old inspector.

"It's easy for you to stand there and laugh. You think you're better than anybody else in the shop."

Joe hitched up his khaki trousers and replied with deliberate anger, "I never claimed that. I just read a little more and ponder a little more than the average fellow. That's why I don't laugh at them, I feel sorry for them. If I'm a little freer, I've had to make sacrifices for it — no dependents, no ties." He added cryptically, "They punish you one way or they punish you another way."

Walter did not quite understand, but it struck him that these remarks were a prelude to farewell.

He asked uneasily, "You're not going to quit?"

"One of these days. Maybe the weather will turn, or I'll hear of something else, or I'll have words with Buster . . ." He added with somewhat more warmth, "But I'll be back — if not here, some place like here. You won't, though. That's why I hope you won't forget what it was like for the people who made the things you'll be buying."

Walter cried indignantly: "How could I? How could I ever forget?" It seemed to him that the thick scurf of silver through which he shuffled as he worked, the glittering waste of lead filings and melted sticks, were so many needles, each carrying its stinging injection of memory — of sweat, exhaustion, harrying, feverish haste, and stupid boredom.

"You forget worse things, don't you? Pain, and even death? You'll think back on the days when you were slaving away to save money for college, and they'll strike you as comical, maybe even romantic."

"God forbid!" Walter laughed. And yet he had suddenly a shivery foretaste of a future beyond the one of which he daydreamed as he worked.

When the siren screamed the end of their nine and a half hours, Walter hurled his file and apron into his toolbox and trotted down the aisle toward the time clock. Turning the corner of the body shop office just as its lights were extinguished, he ran headlong into one of the iron antennae of a fork truck and cried aloud with pain as the metal plate struck his shinbone. Tottering backwards, Walter was sud-

denly gripped by the forearm and pulled erect. He turned
gratefully and found himself staring into the eyes of Joe.

Smarting with soreness and embarrassment, Walter demanded aggressively, "I suppose that's what you want me to
remember!"

A faint stubble glinted along Joe's narrow cheeks. Gray-
ing like his iron hair, it aged him as it grew. He scraped his
hand across it wearily and replied quietly, "Never mind the
machinery. Remember the men. The men make the machines, and they make their own tragedies too. Once your
own life gets easier, you'll take it for granted not only that
theirs must be easier too, but that they deserve what they
get anyway, that some law of natural selection has put you
up where you are and them down where they are."

They had reached the clock bay where they took their
place meekly in line, waiting to punch out, shuffling forward every few seconds while they spoke in low voices.
Around them a swarm of men surged toward freedom —
noisy boys with laughter to spare for the evening; haggard
weary men in their forties; surly powerful black men in
stained coveralls and scrawny brown men chattering in
Spanish; vacant-faced fools with slack jaws and dangling
hands; shrewd-eyed men fingering their union contract
books, composing their campaign leaflets, and computing
their chances of election to positions that would lift them
out of the work routine.

"Why do they stay?"

"They're trapped, that's why. They say everybody's supposed to be, one way or another, but it's worse to be stuck here. Spending your life on the production line means counting out the minutes, being grateful that Mondays go fast because you're rested, and hating Tuesdays because the week is so long. It means that you're paying off forever on all the things you've been pressured into buying by getting up every day in order to do something you'd never, never think of doing if it was a matter of choice. It means never having anything to look forward to in all of your working life." Joe took his card from the rack, clicked it in the time clock, and with a wave of his hand was gone.

What was happening, as Walter woke daily to the dawn's dull alarm and went from the still house through the newly washed streets to the waiting assembly line, was that his self-pity, so strong that the page blurred before him when he lay in bed reading himself to sleep, was altering into a maturer concern with the fate of others who could not, like himself, set a term to their labor.

He began to question the men on the line with him, one after another, to find out how many of them felt as he did about what they were doing for a living. More sure of himself with every passing hour, he moved up and down the line, demanding, whenever there was a moment, an answer to his insistent question: "Do you think anybody likes coming in here to work?"

"Everybody does one day a week — payday," said the solder flower.

"Not even the bosses," said the deck fitter. "Do you think anybody with sense would knock himself out in this dirt and noise if it wasn't for the money?"

And the door fitter said wryly, "Do you know what this kind of work is? It's colored man's work. But even the colored men are smartening up — they turn up their noses at it too unless they get strapped."

Saddened and bewildered by this last comment, Walter turned away from the man who had made it and who had punctuated his bitter remark with a series of thunderous blows on a door that he was fitting. Only Orrin, the second metal finisher, grudgingly admitted that the work was a challenge to him, that the pay was fair, and that there were worse jobs. Behind them all, long-jawed Joe, caught up with his work as usual, stood casually beveling his screwdriver.

"I hear you've been taking a little poll," he said to Walter.

"What's it to you?" Walter asked truculently. He was in no mood to be mocked.

With apparent irrelevance, Joe replied by demanding, "How come you fixed on being an engineer?"

Walter was taken aback. "Why, that's where everybody says the future is."

"That's not reason enough for a fellow to struggle and sweat to get to college. Damn it, doesn't anybody go out and do what he wants to any more? I'm not saying you wouldn't make a good engineer, or that it wouldn't be fine for a change to have some engineers who care as much about people as they do about gadgets. But supposing you find out after you get to college that you want to spend your time learning something useless — are you going to leave yourself open for it?"

"Boy, you sure are free with advice."

Joe looked at him gravely. His long sad jaw had the hint of a smile. "The men on the line like you, Walter. They don't think you're just nosy when you ask questions. They think you're one of them, and in a good way you are. Maybe that's why I've got hopes for you."

Walter fought hard against the influence of the older man, whose crabbed and subversive outlook was so foreign to everything Walter had been taught; but he was forced to admit to himself that more and more he was seeing the factory through Joe's cold, discerning eyes, and he began to fear that if Joe were ever to leave, the plant would have no real existence other than as a money-producing nightmare. Not only was there no one else really to talk to about it, but Joe had forced Walter to try to formulate his emerging ideas in an adult and comprehensible way.

"The worst thing about the assembly line is what it does to your self-respect," he said to Joe early one morning as they squatted on their haunches, waiting for the starting siren. "It's hard to keep from feeling like a fool when you know that everybody looks down on what you're doing, even the men who are doing it themselves."

Joe hung his hammer and metal spoon from the brass hook at his belt. "The big pitch has always been that we're a practical people, that we've proved to all the impractical European dreamers that production can serve people. But instead people are serving production. Look how frightened, how hysterical the bosses get when the line stops — they can't afford to figure what it costs *you* to keep it moving — they only know they've got a production quota. Of course when sales resistance starts building up and they put the cork back in themselves, they give you just the opposite story. Who can blame the poor slob in the middle for suspecting that the whole setup is really as nutty as a fruitcake, and for feeling ashamed of himself for being caught up in it?"

"All right," Walter challenged him. "Who's crazy? You, me, the guys around us, or the board of directors?"

"Anybody who gets suckered into believing that there's anything real behind the billboards they put up to get the show on the road, so that he commits himself to buying the billboard pictures by selling his life on the installment plan. I sympathize with any joker who begins to suspect that the whole world is against him, that he's the victim of a huge conspiracy organized to make his car fall apart before it's been paid off. Doesn't life in the factory seem to be deliberately designed to lower your own self-esteem? What happens when you're knocking down a dent? If you rap it too hard from the inside, you have to file it down that much more, and you hate yourself for it. If you don't rap it hard enough, you only find out after it's moved on down the line, and then you have to hurry up and wallop it again. In either case you hate yourself instead of hating the car, or the invisible man that started up the line." He laughed briefly in anticipation of what he was about to add. "It's like the man that hits his thumb with a hammer while he's hanging a picture — only here he keeps hitting his thumb because they're moving the wall as fast as the union will let them. Who does he yell at every time that ball peen comes down on his nail? Himself."

"I wonder," Walter said slowly, "how many people actually feel that way."

"More than you can count. It's always safe to figure that if you feel something, the world must be full of people who feel the same way. Every sensible man realizes as he gets older that his feelings aren't unique. After all, that's the basis of the best art — the fact that you recognize yourself in it, and all those inner experiences that you'd thought no one else but you could know."

Walter was willing to recognize that he was not the only one to cringe when Buster called him back on a badly done job, to swear at himself for the mistakes that made him fall behind, to realize how he was being trapped into swearing at himself and deflecting his anger from what he did to the way he did it. But it was hard for him to believe that there were others who felt as intensely as he did, who beat their heads against the bars as he did, who dreamed of sunlight and freedom as he did, even though Joe tried to persuade him that the difference was often one of degree, or of his being able to express his feeling in a way that others couldn't. This was one of the questions that Walter was eager to argue with Joe, who moved from one extreme position to another, always mocking, always challenging him to learn what he stood for and to defend it like a man.

"You know something," Walter burst out impetuously one day, "I don't know what I would have done here without you."

Instead of laughing or belittling this praise, Joe's face darkened. The next morning he was not on the line.

By the third day of his absence Walter was beginning to feel as though it had all been a dream, as though he were slipping once again into the awful pit of loneliness, exhaustion, and self-doubting despair. As a last resort he sought out the men on the line to learn what they thought of Joe.

"He's irresponsible," said Pop.

"He's the kind of guy that just don't care," said the younger inspector. "No wife, no kids — no wonder he can take off three days without worrying about getting a reprimand or getting fired."

"He knows his work," said Orrin grudgingly. "I don't know where he learned it, but he did. Just the same, he takes off. You can't *afford* to take off like that nowadays, not if you want to hold down a job."

On the fourth day he came back. He told no one where he had been. "Am I glad to see you!" Walter exclaimed — but Joe merely indicated, with a cold grin and a turn of his tattooed arm, that from time to time things came up that were more important than the making of automobiles.

He did not set to work, but almost immediately was engaged in serious talk with Buster the foreman and with the union shop steward. The two were arguing vigorously, but suddenly Joe cut them off simply by lifting his hand. He said something very briefly, shoved his hands into his pockets, and the discussion was finished.

To Walter's amazement he came back to the line, picked up his toolbox, and nodded casually to him.

"I just quit, Walter," he said. "Going to hit the road."

"But —"

"You'll make out all right, no matter what you do. I don't even have to wish you good luck."

Then he was off down the aisle, on his way to the tool crib and the plant police and the parking lot and God alone knew where after that, without so much as a handshake or an inclination of his lean frame. Suddenly Walter remembered something: "Hey!" he shouted. But Joe — if he heard him — did not turn around and soon was out of sight.

You never told me about Pop, he wanted to tell Joe, you never answered all the questions I was going to ask you — but even if Joe had not gone for good, Walter would not have known how to say to him all the things that should have been said, the words of gratitude and self-confidence.

When the relief man came a few minutes later to give him a twelve-minute break, he hurried to the bathroom. There, just beyond the big circular sink that could accommodate half a dozen men, he could see out the tilted window to the vast parking lot.

The dull winter light was gloomy and deceptive, and so vague was the air that the dark ranks of massed automobiles were no more than darker blurs against the background of the gray steel fencing and the lowering sky. One of the cars moved, or was it his imagination? But no, the red taillight dimmed, glowed, dimmed. Joe, the vanishing American, was swinging out of the lot and away from the production line, out of Walter's life and into someone else's, out of the present and into what lay beyond the gate. He was leaving the future to Walter, who now at last could wave his farewell, with his face pressed to the cool window as he watched the little light disappearing from view.

Then he washed the sweat from his face and returned to his work.

FOUR

A Present for the Boy

AT BOMBER bases and in baseball clubhouses, at fire-house pinochle tables and in logging camps, in coal mines and among sand hogs, in the fo'c'sles of freighters and among the loading gangs at their piers, wherever Americans work, play, or fight, always there is one man known as Pop. Married or single, young or old, expansive or taciturn, he will have been recognized as the senior member of the group, and from then on, regardless of his own will, his life will have acquired a new dimension, unsought and perhaps even unenjoyed.

In the body shop of the auto assembly plant Pop was instantly recognizable, even from some distance, by his foaming shock of white hair, which tumbled over his forehead in a snowy cascade, and gave him a certain dignity even when partly obscured by the cap which usually covered it at an odd angle, its peak jutting out over one ear. This touch of dignity was vitally necessary, for Pop was cursed with a polysyllabic, unpronounceable last name, and stood only an inch or two more than five feet. Wizened and homely, with a cigar permanently suspended, not clenched but dangling, between his sallow lips, he tended to reinforce his resemblance to a small monkey by hopping jaggedly about, grimacing furiously, and shouting unintelligible curses around his flopping, unlighted cigar.

Pop had been working on the line as long as any of the foremen or supervisors in the body shop; indeed, he had been Pop to them even when *they* were working on the line in the old plant in the old days, hanging on during the depression by clambering over the backs of weaker men; and while they remained friendly with him as a fellow member of their Old-timers' Club and thus a sharer of secrets and memories, they could not encourage intimacy with him because of the very fact that he had never become a boss.

Since he was known to everyone — in the duck pond, in the pit, in the grinding booth, in the paint booth, on the jigs, even in the trim department — Pop had been deputized to serve as collector for the weekly check pool. At first he had been uneasy with the responsibility, but once he had learned how to read the last five serial numbers on a pay check as a poker hand, he came to look forward to making the rounds during his relief break on payday, calling out to everyone from whom he had already collected fifty cents, "T'ree eights is high so far. Anybody beat t'ree eights?"

With his cigar dangling before him like a dowsing rod as he hurried along expectantly in search of the lucky man, his snowy sheaf of hair did not float up and down in triumph only because the winner was going to tip him five or ten dollars for his trouble: Pop did not turn down the tip, but more important than the money was the knowledge that once a week he was the bearer of good tidings, the moneyed ambassador sure of a happy welcome from some lucky man whose full house or four of a kind would send him home with double pay in his pocket.

Pop had even been approached to run for office in several union elections, to lend strength to a ticket composed of men who were not as well known in the plant as he. But he had refused, just as he would have turned down a company offer to be made a foreman, because he had a sense of his own limitations; and this modesty, coupled with a native shrewdness that would not allow him simply to be used by those who were more educated than he, earned him popularity if it limited his future.

For many years Pop had lived in a frame two-bedroom house with his wife and their only child (two other children had died in infancy and there had been many miscarriages before the boy had been born and survived). He had bought the house in the very pit of the depression, paying the bank three thousand dollars for it in 1933, partly because he knew full well that it was the buy of a lifetime at that price, and partly for the somewhat more mystical reason that he wanted to prove his immigrant's faith in his country and his industry.

Most of the three thousand dollars was mortgage, but Pop was not used to having debts on his back and he knew how to live cheaply. By the time the auto union had won the NLRB election, it was no longer necessary to have leek soup five times a week, and Pop methodically set aside his wage increases for the amortization of his mortgage. By the time his wife took mortally sick, he owned the house free and clear, and was able to start paying the hospital what he had been paying the bank.

Pop and his wife had never gotten along. The reasons for this were various, and since no one would ever have dreamed of asking him about them — least of all his wife, who took his coldness with the bitter stoicism born of a thousand years of peasant suffering — they remained forever unexpressed. But the agony which was his wife's portion did not leave him unmoved, and as the malignancy swept through her system like a creeping rot, he sat by her side in their bedroom hour after hour, stroking the hand that he had left untouched these many years. Their son Rudy spent those evenings hunched over the kitchen table, doing his homework in algebra, Spanish, and chemistry (subjects whose very names meant nothing to his parents), and in order that his mother's groans might not distract him from his lessons Pop took to talking loudly, sometimes nonsensically but almost continuously, over his wife's gasps of pain.

"You know the inspector on the jigs," he would say. "I told you about Willie, he was complaining to me today they made a nigger an inspector in his section." Seeing his wife twitch on the pillow, gathering her waning strength to retch and groan, he reached for the pot and at the same time went on loudly, "I told him, 'Who are you to kick? You afraid he's going to marry your daughter? You don't want he should feed his family too?' So he said a hunky like me don't understand nothing."

When the doctor lifted his hands despairingly, Pop took his advice and had the ambulance carry his wife, no longer stout and red-faced, to the hospital. After that he and Rudy took turns visiting her in the room where she lay dying with three other women. When Pop went to her, Rudy stayed home and did his schoolwork, then went down to the corner to hang around outside the candy store with his buddies until his father would hop off the trolley car, the cigar hanging limply from his bloodless lips, the cap wilting on his white head. When Rudy went to his mother, taking along a book to read toward the end when she no longer recognized him, Pop stayed home to do the dinner dishes and clean the house.

As is so often the case, his wife was too long in dying, but at last she was gone and decently buried, and Pop, taking the neighbors' muttered condolences with lowered eyes, thanks, and a handshake, was able to sigh with relief and not even to feel guilty at the sigh, for he knew that he had done everything that a husband should. Now at last, he felt, he was entitled to live without the rack of economic pressure or physical torment, and to enjoy his life with the one human being whom he adored — his son.

The pay check which had been gobbled up first by the bank, then by the hospital, now went secretly into a small box for Rudy's college education. There was, besides, the six, seven, sometimes ten dollars that came to him tax-free every week for running the check pool. He had once told Rudy, who was not particularly interested, about how he went around on payday collecting and then disbursing the fifty-cent pieces — but he had not explained that he accepted money for what he did. Obscurely, he had wanted to keep at least one fact of his life secret from his son — not because he saw no need, as in the case of his late wife, to reveal everything about his own private existence, but simply because he sensed the ultimate advantage in having an extra spigot to tap in case both hot and cold faucets should run dry.

"Say," the men on the line would kid him when they saw him paying off the happy winner and in turn pocketing the odd bills that were his due, "what you going to do with all that loot, Pop? Why don't you buy yourself some decent stogies for a change?"

He would merely smile mysteriously, gumming his unlighted cigar, and shoving back the grease-stained old cap to scratch his yellowing hair; thus he betrayed his bewilderment at the effort to indulge in repartee and his genuine lack of knowledge of what he *was* going to do with that money.

It was only gradually, as Rudy proceeded through high school during these happiest years of his father's life, that Pop made the big decision as to how he was going to spend the check-pool money. It pleased him just to sit and think about it, resting his white-stockinged feet on the hassock after work, with one eye on the television and the other on the front door through which Rudy was apt to come bounding in, not like the man who shared the house with him, but more like a well-trained young Airedale or retriever, his blond hair cropped short, his sweater with the big athletic letter unbuttoned part way down, a basketball or a football tucked under his arm, and a gigantic ice-cream cone clutched in his hand.

Rudy was usually out evenings, with his gang down at the candy store or rarely with a girl; it never occurred to him that he was leaving his father alone every night after supper, but then he was always back by ten-thirty, since he was used to keeping training hours. He was twice his father's size, and as invincibly American as the heroes of the movies that Pop occasionally went to see. Pop knew very little about him or his dreams, if he had any, but he observed him minutely at the breakfast table and over the dinner dishes, and sometimes he tiptoed in to watch the young athlete sleeping the sleep of the innocent and the youthful, flat on his well-muscled back with his naked arm

upflung and his mouth ajar just enough to permit the air
to murmur through, and he thought himself the luckiest
man in the world, to live quietly and at peace and even to
share an occasional confidence with this beautiful boy.

For Pop, worn by fulfilling the task of his generation,
the making of countless thousands of automobiles — automobiles stretching from assembly line to highway to
junkyard to steel mill back to assembly line — had finally
yielded to the repeated suggestion that he exchange production work for inspection. In his bones he knew that he was
tired, dog-weary of the endless hours of stooping and banging and squatting and scraping and sweating, and he had
portioned out to himself the remaining weary years of work
until he should be eligible for retirement and Rudy should
be on his own; but if he had been offered an inspection job
only because of all this, his worker's pride would have demanded that he turn it down. The job was finally put to
him as one calling not only for the irreplaceable kind of
experience that was his, but for expert eyesight that would
have to be physically checked in the plant hospital.

Thus challenged, Pop submitted to the eye examination,
passed, and was given a pile of soft cloths and a box of
chalk to replace the polished tools he had worn smooth
and shiny through so many years of constant use. He no
longer had to sweat, but merely to squint at the jobs as they
rolled by; he no longer had to pound, but merely to indicate
with a flick of the chalk between his rheumatic fingers the
places that others were to pound. The years had taught

him where to look and where to feel with the tips of his fingers, and this work was so simply and pleasurably automatic that he was free to think.

So it was that he found himself turning over in his mind, not just in the evenings while he waited for Rudy, but during the day as he bent to his work, what he was going to do with the money that was piling up every pay-day, the extra money that Rudy knew nothing about. Looking around him in the brilliant new factory (he had been one of the old-timers who had survived the moving of the plant from its old location to its immense and magnificent new home), he was struck by the hundreds of strange young faces on the production line. They came and went in a continuous revolution, like boys running in and out of a schoolyard, so that the faces swam before his eyes; except that here when these boys disappeared it was for good, and their replacements were sure to disappear also — and when the sweat ran down their flushed young faces it was for hard-earned money and not for fun.

Many of these boys, especially the tall ones and those with athletic sweaters and crewcut hair, reminded Pop of his Rudy, who was already in his last year at high school and almost ready to be flung out into the world; indeed, he himself would sometimes burst out in a cold sweat when he came upon a big blond youngster bending over the water fountain or adjusting a pair of goggles over his eyes, with the irrational fear that here was Rudy, dropped out of school or casting off larger ambitions as these boys had done, in order to fill out the family income or have money for sharp clothes and nice girls or make the monthly carrying charges on a new car.

That was the point at which Pop got his idea. Looking back on it later, he could trace it to a fear that Rudy would betray him by being satisfied to become a grinder or a buffer or a welder or a metal finisher on the assembly line simply to gratify his immediate material desires, and to a hope that he could head this off by getting for Rudy a graduation present so splendid that it would serve many purposes at once: it would remind Rudy that his father loved him and would do anything for him, it would be a symbol of what you could buy with hard work, and it would by its very presence and existence as *his* make it impossible for Rudy to cut short his education or close out his future on the excuse that he wanted to earn money at once to buy himself an automobile.

There were people who bought their sons automobiles for high school graduation presents. Pop did not know any such people, but he saw pictures of them in the magazines, so he knew that it could be done, even though it would seem wildly extravagant to his own neighbors and friends. Pop didn't give a damn about their opinion — in fact, he looked forward to making their eyes bulge. He went about the whole thing as methodically as he had gone about the buying of the house so many years before.

"Rudy, I been looking at your report card," he said one night when his son came slouching in the door, football in hand and a strawberry-colored bruise high on his right cheekbone.

"What about it?"

"I looked hard, and it ain't good enough."

"Aw," his son said. "What you want, anyway? I passed everything."

"Sit down." He even took the cigar out of his mouth and waved the wet end at his boy. "You think I'm a greenhorn or something, all I got to do is sign it and forget about it? It ain't enough to pass nowadays. Just like it ain't enough to have a high-school education. It used to be, but not any more. Nowadays all you can do with it is go to work on the assembly line."

"What's wrong with that?" Rudy asked boldly. "You're doing it."

Pop glared at him. "Because I don't know how to do nothing else. You got the head to do better, and I'm willing to give you the chance. Now listen. I know you got to have top marks to get into college. You can still do it. You bring home an eighty-five average in June and I'll give you the biggest God damn graduation present of anybody in your whole high school."

He had finished, and he was panting with excitement. It was a long time since he had spoken to Rudy like this, and he could feel the blood in his face. What was more, his son's eyes were glittering, sparkling like butterflies, so brightly that it almost hurt him to look into them.

"What is it, Pop? You got something special in mind?"

"You're damn right. But you'll never find out what it is if you don't do your part. Bring in the marks, and I'll bring in the present. Is it a deal?"

Pop knew it was a deal before he asked. He was so confident that Rudy would strain every nerve to make the required grades that he went ahead at the plant and made preparations for selecting a really good car. First he sought out his friend Louis, an inspector on the final line who checked brakes and shocks.

"Louis," he said to him as they sat in the cafeteria having a coffee before starting time, "Rudy's going to graduate high school in June."

Louis turned toward him his Roman gladiator's broken-nosed face and dug his fingers into his curly gray hair. "I'd swear it was yesterday, the union picnic when Rudy won the sack race for ten-year-olds."

"I want to get a present for the boy."

Mildly interested, Louis sipped his coffee in silence.

"I want to buy him a new car, right off the line."

"Christ!" his friend spluttered, staring at him in dismay. "Have you gone nuts?"

"I got my reasons." He added quietly, "He's a good boy, he deserves it."

"But a *car*. My God, you never bought yourself a new car. Not once, in all these years. Is this one at least going to be for you too?"

Pop shook his head. "Just for the boy. If he goes to college, he takes it with him. You know what it means to a boy, a new car? A convertible? To me it's nothing, I'm an old man, I can drive an old heap, it's all the same to me. So don't argue with me, Louis. I just want to ask you, if I tag a good convertible, one that I know has good fit all over, a good deck-lid fit, doors that close right, will you watch it for me when it comes down the line? See that it don't leak, that the brakes are tight — you know, every- thing."

"Of course I will. But —"

"I'm going to ask Colletti, the foreman over in paint, to keep an eye on it for me. He'll make a mark right next to mine on the tag, and you'll know it's okay when it reaches you."

"All right, sure. If you're going to buy, you're going to buy. How are you going to finance it?"

Pop looked him in the eye. He took out his cigar and said, "I don't believe in that financing crap. Maybe I'm old-fashion, but I don't want to pay four hundred bucks extra for the privilege of owning the car. I saved up for it, Louis. I saved up for it for a long time, and I'm going to pay cash." He put his coffee cup down, pleased at the ex- pression on Louis's face, arose, and headed for his work.

Once he had made his decision, Pop was serene. On the job he retained his payday prerogative of collecting and pay- ing off for the check pool. It meant that he could peer into all the new faces, thrusting his cigar into the uneasy smiles of the probationary men and asking them if they wanted to play the pool while he sized them up, shaking his white mop of hair dubiously at the types of men that were turning up nowadays in the factory. These men were native-born, all of them, except for an occasional DP shyly taking his place in the industrial routine, and even these few were so eager to strike roots that they took on the color of their fellows as quickly as possible, not at all glad even for a brief chat in their native tongue with Pop.

"It's a different kind of guy you see coming in here," he remarked philosophically to Orrin, who had himself been working on the line as a metal finisher for less than a year and who nodded as he lit a cigarette off the blue flame of a solder gun and bent to his rugged work. "When I first started, you wouldn't see all American-born like you do now. They was from all over the four corners of the world. And I'll tell you something more. Those foreigners like me worked harder in them days, not just because there was no union protection and you had speed-up, speed-up all day, but because they figured they had a good job and they wanted to hang on to it and make something out of themselves. These kids coming in now, I watch them, I know what they're like. They figure it's a crumb job, they say it's like the army, and they won't stick it out here a minute longer than they have to. The attitude's different, you know what I mean, kid?"

Orrin spat out loose tobacco and smoke in an angry gesture. The sweat stood out on his balding forehead under his blue-striped railroad cap as he strained to reach a dent high on the hip of his car's quarter-panel. He was a stern-faced man of thirty-five whom you might have taken for a preacher if you had first met him in a dark suit instead of in his blue coveralls, which bore his name embroidered in yellow over the breast pocket and across his back the words, in large block yellow characters:

LAKESIDE

SERVICE STATION & REST.

He straightened up from his work with a grunt. "Damn right I know what you mean. Nobody wants to give a day's work for a day's pay any more. The more you goof off, the more of a hero you are to your buddies. I wasn't brought up like that. I was brought up to work."

Mildly Pop objected, "You're not the only one. Maybe my boy don't work like I did when I was his age, but should he have to? Besides, I taught him you don't get no place without work. No, what I mean is him and his friends, all the young fellows, they look down on work like this here. They don't want to get their hands dirty, they don't want to raise up a sweat, and if they have to they kick like hell about it."

Orrin glanced at him shrewdly. He knew that Pop had picked him to unburden himself to not just because they happened to be standing next to one another, but because Pop knew him to be one of the few who took his work seriously. "I don't see you bringing your son in here for a job."

"God forbid!" Pop cried fervently. "If he couldn't do any better than this —" but then he stopped, struck suddenly dumb by the contradiction into which he had been lured. Jamming the dead cigar between his lips, he caressed the next job on the line with his cloth-covered hand and began to chalk it up, casting a final stealthy look at Orrin. The metal finisher wore a nasty look of triumph about his thin lips, pursed for the job which he was surveying. There was something unpleasant about the man, something that made you regret the impulse that led you to speak to him in the first place: when you thought about it, he looked not so much like a preacher as like a mortician, an undertaker who gloated over each customer not as a matter of business, but because he was still alive, while his client, having lost the battle, was very much dead.

Orrin could not resist a parting jibe. "Take the kid there," he said, nodding at a young metal finisher who was striving furiously, crouched like a baseball catcher before his slowly moving work, to punch out a dent, sweat streaming down his forehead and his lips moving silently — praying, or maybe cursing. "Walter's willing, but he doesn't seem to know the first thing about metal finishing, or about doing any kind of hard work. He doesn't know how to pace himself, he doesn't know when to quit and move on to another job. So he's knocking himself out like a punching bag — he'll be half dead by the time he gets out of this plant. Just the same you've got to give him credit for the old college try. I hear he's saving up to go away to school, did you know that?" He added maliciously, "It isn't every boy you see doing that nowadays."

Relaxing at home with his feet up before the television and his day-long cigar actually lighted, Pop tried to put Orrin's digs out of his mind. When you came down to it, Orrin and Louis and all the rest of them, young and old alike, were jealous. It was a human thing, and there were very few people who could rise above it.

Rudy was staying at home more. He was getting down to the finish line and he couldn't hide the fact that he was scared. He studied hard, lugging home extra books and holding long telephone conversations with studious class-mates whom he had previously scorned. His long, powerful legs sprawled before him and the telephone cocked into his shoulder, he wrote hastily as he listened, nodding, uh-huh-ing, and filling his notebooks. Would he have been able to go into the plant and sweat it out for a year or two in order to earn his own college education like Walter? Not his own car — any damn fool kid could do that, sticking at it till he'd made the payments and then waking up to realize that there was no other way for him to make a living — but his own college education? There was no way of knowing short of forcing him into it, and that was exactly what Pop, star-ing at the boy with eyes swollen with pride and adoration, had no intention of doing.

One day it was all over. Pop came out of the plant with

his lunch box and the morning paper under his arm and was astonished to see Rudy waiting for him at the gate, chatting with a plant policeman. The boy looked like a movie hero, already a little tan, standing there in his short-sleeved sport shirt, more powerful and taller than the cop.

"I made it, Pop," he cried happily. "With room to spare. I got an eighty-seven-point-two average!"

"I figured you would," Pop said calmly. "I figured you'd come through when the pressure was on." He wished that some of his fellow workers would come out, so that he could introduce them to Rudy, but the boy had a quick stride, and Pop had to hurry along to keep up with him.

"Take a look at that new convertible by the gate," he remarked casually to his son. "How'd you like to own one?"

"Man," Rudy sighed. "Who wouldn't?"

"Well, you will. I got one all picked out for you. A beauty. You earned it, kid."

Rudy started to stammer. He turned very red. "But — but — you're kidding!"

"You'll get it in time for graduation. Didn't I promise you something extra special if you made that eighty-five? I ordered it in two tones of blue, your favorite color."

His son was actually trembling, and his eyes were filled with tears of gratitude. "Honest," he said, "I don't know what to say."

"Just say that you'll drive careful and that you'll try to make something of yourself, like you already started to this year."

On the night of the graduation exercises Rudy and his father sat up late, drinking beer on the front porch. The new car, in which they had driven splendidly to and from the school, stood coolly at the curb, dappled in moonlight.

After the second can of beer Pop reminisced, as though it had all happened ages ago, "Sure got a kick out of seeing you on that stage, especially when the principal give you the diploma and said you was President of the High Y and all that."

"That was just because I was good in sports," Rudy replied uncomfortably. Then he started to laugh. "You know something, I haven't seen you so dressed up since Ma's funeral."

"Yes . . . yes . . . I guess that's right." Pop nodded slowly. "She should have been there tonight. . . . Well, look at the time. I still got to get up in the morning and go to work."

Rudy shuffled his feet. "Say, as long as you're going to bed, you wouldn't mind if I went out for a while, would you? I thought I'd drive down to Steve's Place — they say there's a whole mob there celebrating."

Pop arose and put his hand on his son's shoulder. "Go ahead, have a good time. No more football or basketball, you don't have to go to bed early any more, hey?"

"That's right, Pop."

After that Pop hardly ever saw his son. Without the need to be in by ten-thirty, he used to creep back in the dead of night. Sometimes the old hand alarm, which Pop used to weight down his trousers with as they hung from the bureau, read three o'clock, sometimes even later as Rudy tiptoed into the bathroom to undress. When Pop arose and went off to work, he could hear his son breathing heavily and rhythmically behind his closed door. I'll give him a couple weeks to get it out of his system, Pop thought. No use nagging him about it when the car is still so new. But the scene for which he was half-consciously bracing himself never came.

On the Saturday night after graduation, Pop spent the evening playing pinochle with three friends from the plant, and then stayed up to watch the late show on television. He was hopeful that it would knock him out so that he would not lie tensely waiting for the sound of Rudy pulling up to the curb. But even after an extra can of beer he had trouble falling asleep, and when at length he did drop off, towards two-thirty, he slept hard, dreaming of the murders he'd seen and the cards he'd misplayed.

Less than an hour later he was awakened by the shrill peal of the front doorbell. It sounded like someone screaming, a woman screaming, he thought dazedly as he sat upright in bed, the collar of his nightshirt clinging clammily to his neck. Rudy must have forgotten his key, he thought as he struggled to consciousness; but even as he padded barefoot down the stairs, without stopping to look for a bathrobe, he realized that that was impossible, since Rudy had put his house key proudly on the new golden chain with his car keys.

He opened the door and blinked out at the tall policeman bulking before him, his frame outlined by the rays of the street lamp. The policeman held something cupped in his hand that looked like a driver's license, or an identification card from a wallet.

"Casimir Sczystafkiewicz? Sorry I can't pronounce it any better." The policeman bent towards him apologetically, protectively.

"That sounds like me. What's the matter?"

"There's been an accident. Rudolph —"

"Where is he?"

"Sisters of Charity Hospital."

The policeman waited in the parlor in absolute silence while Pop dressed, then held the front door open for him solicitously and slammed it to after checking to make sure that Pop had his keys on him, and led him to the squad car at the curb.

As soon as Pop entered the hospital, which was as familiar to him as a second home, although he had simply pushed it out of his mind in the years since his wife's death, he knew that he had come too late.

Rudy had been dead on arrival, he was informed bluntly. There had been a girl in the car with him who had been thrown clear (he had been pinned behind the wheel when he rammed a concrete abutment at fifty miles an hour) and who was now bleeding internally. No prediction could be made about her chances to her parents, whom he had passed crying furiously in the otherwise empty waiting room.

Pop looked down wonderingly at his son, sheeted to the chin. Only a small bruise, like the old football souvenirs, outlined the closed right eye. He felt everything toppling within him, finally and forever. He touched the boy's crisp hair, still damp with the sweat of shock, and turned away toward the door, unable to control the noises that welled up in his throat as though he were being strangled.

"You got somebody to keep you company?" The policeman held him by the elbow.

"No. Nobody. That's all right," he said, freeing himself. "I'll be all right."

"You want me to take you back home?"

"I guess so." Pop looked up at him vaguely. "Listen, where's the car?"

"At the scene of the accident. They're taking pictures and drawing sketches, but it'll have to be towed away soon, before traffic starts to build up. We'll notify you about it."

"Can you let me see it?"

The policeman glanced at him queerly. "Sure, it's on the way back."

When they arrived at the scene of the accident, a tow truck was already backed up to the rear end of Rudy's car, and the driver was attaching a tow chain to the spotless chrome bumper. Sand had been scattered over the stains of spilled blood and oil on the asphalt street, but the abutment was broken and would be until it was rebuilt, and the automobile was smashed beyond rebuilding. The steering wheel, on which his son had been impaled, was straight and rigid as a harpoon, pointing mutely toward the roof of the car.

"How . . ." Pop hesitated. "Do you know how it happened?"

"They were drinking. Not drunk," the policeman added hastily as he started up the squad car, "but drinking. Seems like he was blinded by approaching lights — he was going too fast anyway — and he got rattled and twisted the wheel too hard."

The policeman waited at the curb until Pop had entered his house and turned on the lights; then he drove off into the night. Standing at the window behind the porch, Pop watched him disappear. Then he sat down and waited for the dawn.

When the sky was blue enough for him to turn off the lights, he telephoned his parish priest, who was preparing for early Mass. Then he went into the kitchen to heat the pot of coffee that he had left on the stove for his son, and, automatically drinking the scalding brew as he stood at the stove, he waited for the people to come and for the arrangements to be made.

The next day was Monday. He arose at a quarter to six and made two sandwiches and a Thermos of coffee for his lunch, and left for work. He did not go into the cafeteria, where his friends would be gathered over coffee, but went directly from the locker room and the time clock to the production line itself, deserted except for Buster the foreman, who stood at his desk making out his attendance sheets. His mouth opened when he saw Pop.

"For God's sake," he said, his voice unnaturally loud in the quiet shop, with the line and the machinery not yet running, "what are *you* doing here?"

Pop put a fresh cigar in his mouth. "You heard about it?"

"Louis called up your boss, Halstein, yesterday, and Halstein called me. Christ, Pop, I don't know how to tell you how I feel."

"Yeah, yeah," Pop muttered.

"Say, here comes Halstein," Buster said with relief, pointing to the aisle down which the inspection department foreman was hastening, his bald head gleaming under the fluorescents, his swinging forearms below the turned-back cuffs of his white shirt thick with coarse black hair.

"Hello, Halstein," Pop said around his cigar.

Halstein stuck out his hairy hand. "My condolences, Pop. My wife's too. We were shocked when Louis phoned us yesterday. I never expected to see you here this morning, I was going to come up and see you after work."

"Listen, they got him laid out, Rudy, in the funeral parlor. I can't hang around there, I can't hang around the house. I figured the best place for me is here."

"Well, sure," Halstein said, "but the funeral and everything —"

"They're going to bury him tomorrow morning. I thought I'd take the whole day off, if it's all right with you."

"You don't have to ask that. You can take the week off if you want."

"No . . . no . . . that's not for me. I got to have something to do. Besides, that would have to count as my vacation time, and I know you got the vacation schedule all set up, and it would throw you off if you had an extra man out."

"Matter of fact," Halstein said uneasily, "I wouldn't be able to get away myself for the funeral tomorrow. But I thought Mae and I would stop around tomorrow night."

All that week the men did come to see him, the older men, those he had worked with in the plant for years and years. Some came with their wives, bringing home-baked cakes and cellophane-wrapped baskets of fruit; and everybody in the department, including the newcomers, had chipped in to send a handsome wreath for Rudy's coffin.

It helped to take the curse off the first week. But after that of course they would stop coming, except for the small crowd with whom Pop always played pinochle and drank beer. And Pop would have time on his hands, time in which to think, and to go over and over again what he had done to Rudy with the money he had saved for him.

At the end of the week, on payday, one of the younger metal finishers on the line approached Pop, who was staring off into space with the brown cloth dangling from his hand and the cigar dangling from his lips, and said diffidently, "Say, Pop, are you going to make the rounds for the check pool today?"

Pop looked at him and shook his head curtly. "I been

doing it long enough. It ain't worth the trouble to me any more. You want a check pool, get somebody else to run around."

The boy backed off, hurt written on his face, and Pop was surprised to feel, instead of shame, a stab of pleasure at the boy's discomfiture, the first pleasure he had experienced in a long time.

The question of blame was with him day and night. He slept little, and he went about his work as mechanically as if he were a part of the moving assembly line itself. He had never consciously blamed his wife for not having filled his house with children, as he had been entitled to expect that she would — he had simply stopped caring about her. Now he found that he was caring less and less about himself; he was shaving only when he caught sight of his face in the mirror, changing his socks and underwear only when he bathed, even eating less and not bothering to put away half-finished cans of salmon and torn packages of sliced bread. But he could not bring himself to believe, turn it about in his mind as he would, that he was to blame for Rudy's death.

If he had not made Rudy work and study so hard for the present, maybe he wouldn't have stayed out late every night after graduation. But that was pointless: Rudy could have gotten killed in the car without staying out late. If he had bought Rudy something else, anything else but two hundred and twenty-five horsepower worth of destruction, maybe Rudy wouldn't have held a fatal steering wheel in his hands. But that was pointless too: Rudy was the kind to go out and buy his own car, and get killed in it too, probably. If he had brought Rudy up differently — not to drink, not to drive too fast — maybe he would still be alive and preparing for college. But that was even more pointless: a man who worked hard all day didn't deliberately go out and teach his son wrong things; if Rudy learned wrong, he had learned wrong from his friends, from the movies, not from his father.

Once he had absolved himself of direct guilt, however, there remained the question of whether he had had the right to buy Rudy the car at all. Did a man have the right to buy his son a hunting rifle? Nobody said no, but all sorts of questions could be raised as to what kind of boy he was and consequently what sort of chances there were that he would shoot himself with the gun.

It kept coming back to the question of what kind of boy Rudy had been, and there grew within Pop the terrible feeling (all the more terrible because it made him feel rotten for harboring it) that Rudy had been an unworthy son — unworthy of the automobile, unworthy of his father's love and trust and admiration, unworthy of the innocent girl whom he had crippled. Worthy, in fact, only of squandering his father's life savings as a college bum, only of being representative of his generation, of the careless and wise-talking young men whom Pop saw about him every day.

He realized that he had no patience with the boys who

worked on his assembly line, but he had no desire to curb his impatience. Young Walter in particular, with his short-cut hair and his stubby nose, a kind of poor, sawed-off imitation of Rudy, got on his nerves with his sweat and his lousy, miserable work and his burning ambition to save money and go to college.

One day Walter lunged forward with his file at a hump way down on the rocker panel of his job, a hump that it wasn't even his business to file down, and succeeded only in tipping over a paper cup underneath the line in which Pop kept soaking several sticks of chalk to keep them smooth and workable.

"Can't you watch where you're pushing that file?" Pop demanded, taking the cup and chalk from Walter's clumsy gloved hand.

"I'm sorry, I'm didn't mean to —"

"Sorry — all you guys are sorry after you've made a mess of it. It's a wonder they pull any production here at all with the kind of kids they hire to do a man's job."

Miserable and furious, the boy turned away. But there were others to annoy Pop, and after a time he began to suspect that they were deliberately ganging up on him, not just erasing his chalk marks — as anybody would do if he could get away with it — but dipping his rags in adhesive cement when he wasn't looking, pushing his toolbox around so he couldn't find it, even tattling to his relief man that he was complaining about being gypped out of his time. He was sure that they were whispering about him and nudging each other when he showed up, that they called him a crab and a sourpuss and worse.

"Why don't you lay off Walter and the other kids, Pop?" Orrin demanded one day. "What good does it do you, picking on them?"

"They're picking on me," Pop replied shortly, knowing even as he said it that he sounded petulant and childish.

The fact was that he was getting frightened. Retirement, which he had always thought of as something to look forward to, now loomed before him in all its majestic loneliness like an alp before a weary mountain climber. He would be sitting on his porch with the morning paper and nothing ahead of him for the whole day, while all these young stinkers would be working on the line, sweating maybe, but laughing and making plans for the future and coming home to something every night.

There was a lot, he realized, in what Orrin said, especially when it came from the one man on the line who held himself superior because he knew how to work harder than the youngsters. In the two and a half years that Pop had left on the line he ought to be able to wind up friends with the kids, to have them punching him on the back instead of tripping him up. It's what comes from living alone, he thought, you get a little nuts; and he determined to find company to share the house in which he was going to spend his retirement.

But it could not be a grownup, not a man or a woman whose chatter he would have to listen to night in and night out; and a child was out of the question. For a while he toyed with the idea of buying some dwarf fruit trees and planting them in the little grass strip between his house and that of the Casprczaks next door and watching them grow. But even his wife's tiger-lily border at the side of the house, that she had planted just before her final illness, annoyed him as he brushed past it, perhaps because it reminded him of her, and he knew beforehand that he would sooner sit dreaming in front of the television than be bothered with pruning, spraying, and watering. Finally he stopped in at a pet shop on his way home from work one night and bought himself a mutt.

He did not want a full-grown beast that was set in its ways, that would not respond to a name he would select for it, that would roll over and die of old age just when he needed its companionship in the long days of his retirement. He picked a small dog that was friendly and that had room to grow.

At first he kept the pup locked in the house, but he found that when he returned from work it had ignored the papers he spread on the kitchen floor next to the stove. So he chained it up in the little yard, but then the neighbors complained that it half choked itself by running around in circles and they had to climb in and unwind it. At last Pop hit on the solution. He bought double-thickness aluminum screening and set to work screening in the left side of his porch.

He found that he was starting to talk to the dog as

though it were human and could reply, and for a while he was embarrassed — suppose somebody should hear? — but after a time he grew indifferent: he had been talking to himself for so long that it seemed only natural to talk to the dog.

"Building you a nice home, pup," he would grunt as he hammered the frame into place for the screening. "Lots of fresh air, fresh water, you can crap in the corner. Okay?"

The dog was friendly, and grateful for small favors. When the porch was done, it moved in as though it had always belonged there. Peering at him through shaggy black brows remarkably like Pop's own mop, except for the color, it tried eagerly to anticipate his desires.

"You know what I'm going to call you from now on?" Pop demanded, as he picked up his lunch box and prepared to leave for work. "I'm going to call you Rudy, in memory of a nice boy. He went away and left me all alone, but now I've got you, haven't I? Down, Rudy, down! Now be good and don't try to tear the screening — if you're real good and do your business on the paper like you're supposed to, I'll bring you home a surprise tonight."

Amazingly, the dog leaped up and began to lick Pop's hands.

"Say, you are a smart one, aren't you? You want to know what the surprise is, don't you? Well, I can't tell you, or it won't be a surprise. But if you're good and do like Pop says, you'll get something you like. Remember now!"

The old man slammed his newly made porch door firmly

and backed down the walk, his eyes fixed on his dog, which had clambered up on an old chair and was panting and woofing gently against the aluminum screening.

"Got you where I want you now, Rudy. You won't break loose from there, you'll be waiting when I come home. And don't forget, if you do like I say there's going to be a juicy present for you . . ."

He walked backwards all the way to the corner, thinking of the nourishing and safe soupbone that he was going to pick up from the butcher on the way home, and then, satisfied that the dog was still sitting obediently where he had left it, he turned and shuffled off through the brilliant, blinding streets. At the intersection he put a fresh cigar between his lips, and, as the morning sun struck him full and blazed on his white hair defiantly foaming forth from under the wrinkled cap, he pulled back his shoulders and headed directly into its brightness towards the factory.

Ford Motor Company's Mahwah Assembly Plant in northern New Jersey. Constructed in 1955 as part of Ford's postwar revitalization program, Mahwah turned out Fords and Mercurys in its early years. At its peak the factory employed upwards of 5,000 workers, but the company closed it during the auto depression of the early 1980s. (Ford Motor Company)

The trim line in a mid-1950s Ford assembly plant. Here the glass, lights, and other fixtures are added to the body of the car. As a metal finisher, Harvey Swados prepared auto bodies for this stage of assembly. (Ford Motor Company)

The body drop where the chassis and motor are mated to the body shell.
(Ford Motor Company)

Harvey and Bette Swados at their home in Valley Cottage, New York, in June 1959. Harvey holds an issue of *Dissent*. (Swados family)

Harvey Swados in the early 1970s. (University of Massachusetts Library)

FIVE

On the Line

WHEN Orrin had been working on the line for about a year, his right hand began to stiffen. Instead of letting up, he tightened his grip on his tools and set to work even harder than before. Orrin was a stubborn man; he knew that he had been called a fanatic, and he took a certain pride in the knowledge.

Once, at the height of the auto production season, the men in the body shop were asked if they would come in not only on Saturday, but on Sunday also in order to meet the quota. Although they were entitled to double time for Sunday work, most of them were satisfied with the fifty hours' pay they had already earned, and one of the welders protested bitterly to Orrin.

"Now they want you to work on Sundays, for Christ's sakes. You don't even get to see your family. Are you going to come in, or are you going to tell them you have to go to church?"

Orrin held out his hands to the man, his fists loosely clenched.

He replied coldly, "I never go to church. Work is my religion."

When he saw the look on the welder's face, Orrin wished that he could have taken back the prideful, boasting words. But it was too late, and he knew that it would get around the shop, what he had said and the way he had acted, and it would be added to the already uncomplimentary picture most of the men had of him.

Orrin would have preferred to be liked, but he really didn't care. The men on the line came and went. What the transients thought of him made absolutely no difference. As for the others, the few who like himself made up the permanent backbone of the body shop, they had learned to take him as he was.

At first, when they observed the concentrated fury with which he worked, they muttered, "Company man," and one or two even approached the shop committeeman to find out if the union could get him to slow down. But they soon found out that Orrin did not work the way he did because he wanted to impress the bosses or because he was a brownnose by nature; although he had never belonged to a union before, he was perfectly willing to go along with everyone else on the line, even with their work standards — he was simply used to working hard and steady, and he took his pleasure from the plain fact that he could work better and harder and longer than anybody else around him.

Or so everyone came to understand. While he was not openly sneered at, Orrin knew as the months passed that he was not going to be liked here in the auto plant any more than he had been in the army or in any of the jobs he had held in the years between the end of the Second World War and his coming to work here. He made some casual friends, he earned respect for his severity and his skill and his fortitude, and finally he achieved a kind of neutral balance on the line. This was enough.

Orrin had always despised those who were physically his equals or better but who could not keep up with him; it had been so when he was nineteen and number-one man in his infantry outfit, and it was so now when he was losing his hair but was still number-one man on this line. When he listened to the big young fellows around him whining about how hard their work was, he could not keep the contempt he felt from showing in his face.

In a way it was paradoxical that he, as the one man who really enjoyed pressure, the one man who never complained when the cars moved so fast that they seemed to be rolling on their own fiendish motorless power or so close together that you could hardly squeeze between them to do your job, should have been the one who smiled the least. Those who bitched and those who griped often found occasion to laugh. They pulled practical jokes on each other like children, cutting off the gas to the solder flower's line, cutting off the air to the metal finishers' grinding discs, hiding each other's screwdrivers, rolling heavy buffing wheels like bowling balls down the aisles to bang one another in the shins; but not Orrin. He took his pleasure without showing it, he knew that they must envy him for being able to enjoy what he did without horsing around, and he smiled almost as seldom as he laughed.

As a result Orrin, whose face was long and rather pinched anyway, with two unhumorous vertical lines framing his thin hyphen of a mouth like parentheses, always looked sobersided. He wore a blue-striped railroad man's cap, in which his wife had taken a tuck, to protect his narrow balding head from dust, and baggy coveralls (still advertising LAKESIDE SERVICE STATION & REST., although no one but Orrin knew where it was) which hinted at an undertaker's figure, sad and lean but paunchy. When he changed in the locker room from the coveralls to the dark, conservative suit and tie he invariably wore to and from work, he looked even more like a mortician. Behind his back — he had heard it once — the youngsters called Orrin "The Gravedigger."

Nevertheless, inside he burned. He burned with the fire of youth, and he felt that those around him were no more men than the gutless boys who had come and gone, wounded, weary, or fleeing before the enemy in the French forest where he had fought for one hundred and seven days, senior man in his outfit at the age of nineteen. They groaned about coming in to work at all; they spat with disgust as the siren blew and they had to pick up their tools: it was all too much like the men in his company who had behaved as though Hitler was personally picking on them, when they would have preferred to stay home and let the enemy do as he pleased. For himself, Orrin faced each day with the conviction that he was setting an endurance record, not unlike the one he had set in France. After he had been invalided out of the line against his will, he was awarded an official commendation; at the bottom of his heart he felt that his unblemished attendance and punctuality record on this line would one day be recognized too.

He had always admired, ever since childhood, the flag-pole-sitters and marathon-dancers, the frozen explorers and solo fliers — all those who were able to clench their teeth and carry on indefinitely. His wife had even teased him about it early in their marriage when she learned how Orrin as a schoolboy had studied the box scores faithfully and tensely every day of Joe DiMaggio's marvelous consecutive-game hitting streak.

"I think you cared more about that hitting streak than you did about your own family," Edith had laughed, but then had quickly stopped when she saw his face.

"You don't understand," he had said, as calmly as possible. "Most women wouldn't. It's what makes a man unusual, doing something nobody else can do. It's why I was the last guy to stick it out on the line. They had to carry me back on a stretcher, did you know that?" But then it was his turn to stop, seeing by the expression on her face that she knew all right, knew so well that even though she would never understand, she was bored by the most important thing he'd ever done.

Orrin was driven to try to explain what it had been like, on the line, to men in the factory who cared no more about it than Edith. His fellow veterans cherished reminiscences of Calvados and cognac, of sudden dark encounters and complaisant girls, and they resented being reminded of the unpleasant things, which a lot of them hadn't even lived through anyway, but had only read about in the comfort of their heated barracks.

"Is that all you think about?" demanded Harold the pick-up man, one lunch hour as they were sitting in a semicircle on the floor, eating sandwiches. Aside from an annoying habit of handing out gratuitous advice, Harold was one of the more popular of the older men. He swallowed a small cookie, his large, pointed Adam's apple working up and down like a bobbin as he masticated, and then said: "In point of fact, I was considerably older than you and I was already married when I went off to the army. But that's past history, Orrin. People don't want to hear about it any more."

Stung bitterly, Orrin shot back, "Sure, you probably can't even remember getting hit. You were probably in a drunken fog."

There was an awful silence. Most of them knew that Harold was a drunkard — he had volunteered the information himself in a detached, almost scientific way — but for that very reason no one before had ever dared to mention it aloud.

Harold said coolly, "As a matter of fact, I was cold sober when I earned my Purple Heart. I got sprayed in the ass on Guadalcanal, bending over to pick up a booby-trapped bottle of Jap beer." When the laughter had subsided he added, "But I'm going to be forty years old come my next birthday, and I've got more to think about than that stuff that nicked me way the hell and gone back in 'forty-four.'"

Orrin was left with the boys recently out of high school, who didn't know what war was like and didn't know what work was like. At that only one of them, the kid named Walter who was saving up to go away to college, seemed willing to make the effort to understand. He was clumsy and slow to catch on, but he had a way of gritting his teeth that made Orrin suspect that he would stick no matter how miserable Buster made it for him. What's more, he would stick the way Orrin would have stuck if he'd found it hard: not because he had been starving, or his mother needed money for an operation, but simply as a point of honor.

So Orrin said to him, "Very few people take anything seriously but their own little pleasures. But it's the few that count. They're the ones that win the wars and keep production going."

"Yes, but in a democratic country you have to count on the majority, not just on those few," Walter replied, wiping his red, sweating freckled face against the already wet sleeve of his khaki shirt. "If we dropped dead tonight, the factory would open just the same tomorrow morning, and they'd turn out just as many cars."

Orrin shook his head. "There's always what they call key men. I don't care where it is, if those key men don't hold their end . . . things will fold. Take me. I'm no superman, far from it, but at least I know how to hold on. I'm not saying I won the war singlehanded or any of that boloney, but we would have been a lot worse off in my sector if I hadn't made up my mind I was going to stick it out on the line until they ordered me back or I got hit. And that's what happened. Guys came and went, they got hit, they went batty, they took off like rats, they faked everything from trench foot to clap. But I was there a hundred and seven days, and the longer I held out the more it bucked up the rest of the guys, and that's why I got my commendation after they took the shrapnel out of my legs."

"Those must have been the greatest days of your life," Walter said innocently.

"Well, they were," Orrin replied sharply. He pulled on his gloves and prepared to go back to work. "I don't mind looking back on them — why should I? I don't forget all the mud and slop and blood, or the stinking K rations and C rations, or shaving out of my helmet with cold water. That was part of the whole show. If there's no obstacles, there's no glory, right?"

Walter scuffed his feet through the debris before them, remains of sandwich wrappings, paper bags, cigarette packages, metal filings, stumps of lead. He seemed to be considering an answer. Finally he said, "I guess your life hasn't been very interesting since then if you think about the war so much."

Orrin felt his face getting red. Nervously he yanked off his cap, then jammed it back low on his forehead, so low that it almost covered his eyes. "It's different," he said. "When you're married and raise a family it's different."

"How many kids you got, Orrin?"

"Three. All girls." He took up his file and said aggressively, "Besides, that's what I like about this place. Never mind the money, aside from the fact that the rate is better here than you can get anyplace else. It's a challenge. It's not for sissies and it's not for old ladies. There's always obstacles, they keep the pressure on you all day from the time you punch in, the line keeps going like the tides or the earth turning, and it's up to you to keep up. Once you're on the line, it's up to you." And he went back to his job.

But the boy's question about the rest of his life was like a ladle stuck into a simmering stew — it set Orrin to thinking all over again. He was not happy at home. He couldn't put his finger on it; all he knew was that he looked forward to going to work more than he did to going home.

He had come home from overseas in '45 to the farm town where he had grown up. Everybody on Main Street had given him a big hello, and he had been invited to talk at a chicken dinner given for the GI's. Halting but not shy, he had spoken frankly of those climactic three months of the war when he had stuck it out on the line. His attitude had been so unusual that Mr. Haskins, who owned the feed and grain store, asked him about it.

"Tell me something, Orrin," he had said. "You're the only boy I know that's come back with a good word for the army. If you liked it so much, how's come you didn't re-enlist?"

"No sense being in the army if there's no fighting going on, Mr. Haskins," Orrin had replied. "Besides, I've got a girl. I doubt if I could talk her into marrying a soldier."

Edith was the kid sister of his high-school buddy. Soon after her brother was discharged he had become a television repairman and started to put on weight. He turned out to be a fanny-pincher, the kind of man who was forever bragging about the hot reception he got from the lonely housewives whose antennas he mounted. But Edith was not at all like her brother. What attracted Orrin to her most of all was her intensity.

She was a slim, tallish girl, almost lean, bold-eyed, with ropelike veins in her forearms that protruded even more when she knotted her fingers together in moments of excitement. Although she was not conventionally attractive, Orrin was desperate to make love to her, perhaps because he could sense intuitively the depth and ferocity of her response. She was not the kind to hold him at bay: he had her two or three times in his dad's barn, and once even on her parents' bed, and the more he took her the more anxious he was to marry her quickly and keep her as his own.

Soon after the wedding they moved into a Quonset hut

on the edge of the state college campus and Orrin enrolled in ag school under the GI Bill. Their days were dull and cramped; their nights were agonizingly wonderful. Clamped together on the studio couch under the arching metal roof, they grappled back and forth over tearing sheets, groaning and crying out in ecstasy, the floor around them a tangle of blankets, textbooks, and underclothing. Before the year was out Edith was pregnant.

She wanted above everything, even above success for Orrin, a healthy baby, and she decided that they would have to play it safe. What was more, Orrin's father had been failing on the farm; a fatal disease had wiped out most of his inadequately insured cattle, and he had finally gone to work as a machinist in a soft-drink bottling plant. Within two years he was forced to sell out the farm Orrin had been counting on, and Edith became pregnant again, unexpectedly.

"There's no sense our sticking around here," Orrin said to her one evening after she had put their daughter to sleep in her crib. "We've got no farm to go to. If we have to start from scratch, it might as well be in something with a future. I'm not going to be a farmer, Edie — it's a dying game. Let's pull out."

She sat on the edge of the mattress, winded from having pulled the studio couch apart and made up the bed. Her shoulders sagged; below her sunken chest her belly jutted out like a great globe; her thickly veined hands lay limply across her widespread knees. She grinned up at him, a cigarette dangling from one corner of her mouth. "Better to find out now than later on."

They moved back to her parents' house, into the attic bedroom. Their second daughter was born, and Orrin took a temporary job as a driver for the soft-drink firm where his father worked. The hours were long and the pay was ridiculous; Orrin was relieved when Edith herself suggested that he get the hell out of there and look for a decent job.

After a while — too long for his own comfort, with his father-in-law watching him out of the corner of his eye — Orrin caught on as a roofer's helper. This too paid next to nothing, but at least the government matched his earnings with on-the-job trainee checks. And there was a possibility that in time he might get set up on his own.

But the babies, noisier than little girls are supposed to be, were growing fast, and it was becoming impossible for them to stay on in his in-laws' attic. For the first time, Orrin sensed that Edith was starting tentatively to withdraw from the wholehearted commitment she had made to him during their very first nights together. He couldn't charge her with it, since it never came all the way up to the surface, and Edith went about the household routine as though nothing had changed. Nevertheless he knew absolutely that she was coming to be disappointed in him. He could feel it even in the different way she held him and closed her eyes in their most intimate moments together, and it was galling.

There were no houses to be had that year (or the year before or the year after). It was Edith's mother who finally found them the flat behind the church with which she was affiliated; just knowing how hard she'd had to work on her minister and his board to get them the rooms was enough to make Orrin clench his teeth. He cursed himself to his face while he shaved, observing with contempt how his hair was falling out, and thinking how eager his mother-in-law must have been to be rid of them.

The apartment behind the old white church was rent-free — there were even wages with it — but there was so much work to do in return that it was out of the question for him to hold on to his old job. The church itself had to be reroofed, for a start; the minister's drive had to be graded and graveled, the windows of his study had to be rehung and reputtied; the aisles of the church had to be mopped regularly, the sidewalks shoveled, the metal announcement board redleaded and repainted, the lawns mowed and trimmed. Orrin had become a handyman.

During the years that Orrin held the sexton's job he took on extra work here and there around town — hanging gutters and leaders, digging out septic tanks, installing automatic washing machines. Edith had become somewhat settled, now that she had her own place and her own two little girls; she was not quite so taut, although she remained ambitious for a better life for the four of them. She hinted strongly that she would be willing to get out and push Orrin's career, the way girls did that she knew — except that Orrin had no career.

He began to shop around. He wanted to make a move as

badly as Edith, but he didn't want anything undemanding. "Being a sexton is strictly for an old man," he told his wife, "not for a young guy like me. There's nothing in it to drive you ahead."

Against his better judgment, he joined the local Legion post. As he had suspected, they talked politics and women — two subjects that bored the pants off him — and most of them were men who had no right to belong to the same organization as men who had been in combat. But it was in the Legion bowling alley that he got wind of the gas station partnership deal, so he had no reason to begrudge the dues he paid.

As soon as he was sure that the deal was open, and without telling Edith, he put his name down on the new housing development that was to go up not far from the service station itself. He could handle a GI mortgage, and on the ten-thousand-dollar model the down payment was negligible. Nevertheless he was uneasy, and he waited until the girls were soundly sleeping to talk to his wife. It was very quiet. Beyond their wall the choir was practicing hymns.

"The two-bedroom units are going up fast," he said. "We can move into one without waiting for the gas station deal to jell. If it falls through, so what? The worst that can happen is that I'll have to find another job."

Edith leaped up with that extraordinary agility she had when there was something she wanted to do in a hurry and flung herself onto his lap, her skirt flying up over her thighs. She yanked his tie down and ruffled his thinning hair.

"Tell me about the gas station, Orrin," she said excitedly. "I want to hear all about it — I know this is going to be it at last."

"It's called the Lakeside Service Station and Restaurant. It belongs to George Werlitz's uncle, who's getting too slow for a fourteen-hour grind between the gas pumps and the diner. What he wants is a younger fellow as a kind of junior partner that'll sooner or later buy him out."

"We don't know anything about running a diner. Is it a good spot?"

"It's on Route Ninety-three. All the people that want to go fishing at the north end of the lake have to go by there. And we can learn, can't we?"

Shortly after they had moved into their new house, Orrin took out a GI loan to establish himself as a partner in the Lakeside Service Station and Restaurant, and Edith took over main charge of the diner.

She liked the pressure almost as much as he did, and she was needed just as badly; nevertheless, deliberately this time, she became pregnant again. It was a gamble, and they both knew what she was gambling on. But, for the third time, Edith was delivered of a girl. Freshly shaved and scrubbed, Orrin arrived at her bedside and found her with her face turned to the wall; even after he had greeted her with an intimacy that was somewhat forced because of the eagerly listening mother at the other end of the semiprivate room, she refused to face him, but spoke in muffled tones, holding the bed sheet to her lips.

"What's the matter, Edie? I just saw the baby, it's cute as any I ever saw."

"It's a she. I suppose you're going to pretend you don't care."

Orrin would have been embarrassed even if he had been alone with his wife. He said placatingly, "I love the kids. You can't have a world without girls in it."

Edith twisted about convulsively. Ignoring her gaping roommate, she said loudly, "Don't hand me that crap. It's a man's world. I always wished I was a man. Now I can't even have a son." She began to sob. "What's the matter? Don't you know how to make boys?"

Orrin walked away. At the door he said, "Take care of yourself. I'll be back tonight after I close up."

Actually her bitter question was one he would have asked *her,* if he had dared. That was why she must have burst out at him, partly, to forestall him. She did not mention it again, nor did he, until after he had finally bought out old Werlitz and they were on their own at last, in their own home, with their own business. Edith had plunged back into the affairs of the diner as though she did not have three small children to care for; the life of business seemed to draw her now as Orrin's arms had drawn her in their first days together. She was happy, it seemed to him, even though by nightfall she was groggy with exhaustion; and when they turned off the floodlights and went to bed for their six hours' rest, she curled up dopily in his arms like a child kept up past its bedtime.

But then the blow fell. Without warning the state highway department announced that Route 93 was going to be straightened for a stretch of some twelve miles. When the job was done, the Lakeside Service Station would be standing on a semiabandoned country road, without a quarter of the traffic necessary to keep it solvent. And there was nothing that could be done.

In a blind rage Orrin raced over to old man Werlitz's and pounded on his front door; but his wife said that he was in bed with bursitis. She swore that he hadn't known of the road change when he had sold out. His nephew George, Orrin's Legion buddy, was equally positive that his uncle would never pull such a trick.

"It's the breaks of the game, Orrin."

"But I'm ruined," he cried. "Don't you see that? The oil company might finance me onto the new highway if they wanted to, but I'm tied up with the diner and all that land. How could I take on a new mortgage if I won't be able to liquidate this one?"

George's sympathy amounted to an arm around his shoulders, but that was all. As for Edith, she was unwilling even to give him that much. She only stared at him in cold despair.

"If you'd had your wits about you, you would have known the old man was getting ready to pull a swifty. I told you his price was too good to be true, didn't I?"

"You told me." He laughed shortly. "You've been in this just as deep."

"That's because I wanted to show you what I could do."

"You showed me already. You and your three girls."

"I knew you'd hold it against me for the rest of my life." She rubbed her hands together tautly; the veins began to coil at her wrists. "What good would it do you to have a son? You wouldn't have anything to pass on to him anyway. Except a bunch of debts."

It was after this that Orrin had realized that he and Edith were never going to have any more children, and that he was going to be years in crawling out from under the mountain of debts with which he had saddled himself. Without consulting Edith, he sold out the business and got himself two jobs: one on the assembly line at the new automobile plant, the other working evenings and Saturdays at a lumberyard, loading orders onto trucks for the following morning's deliveries.

He liked both jobs: the assembly line because he felt that once again, for the first time since the war, his endurance and his courage were being tested continually and found up to the mark; the lumberyard because it was startlingly quiet after the thunderous factory, his footfalls echoing emptily in the dimly lighted yard as he clumped about in his steel-toed shoes with the yellow order forms in his hand, balancing kegs of nails on one shoulder, swinging out ten-foot molding strips and swaying sheets of plywood.

Besides the extra pay check, he was able to buy lumber

at wholesale for the dormer-windowed bedroom he was building in the expansion attic on Sundays for the two older girls. This too he was doing without consultation, for there were a jumble of things he wanted to show Edith, not simply to discuss with her: that they were not only not going to lose the house, but were going to make it a bigger and better one; that he was tough enough to handle three jobs at once; and that he cared enough about his daughters to want to make their life more comfortable.

Edith watched him in silence. She had never been much for small talk, any more than he; it was not easy to guess how she felt about his having gone from businessman to factory worker. Once she did say: "There's no point in your killing yourself, Orrin," but when he had replied sharply, "I'm healthy," she had simply commented, "I want you to stay that way. You don't prove anything by doing everything at once."

That was how things stood when his hand began to stiffen. He said nothing about it to anyone, figuring that it came from the use of muscles that had been inactive, just as a man's calves will ache when he attempts to walk after having done nothing but drive for years. He took it as a new test of his fortitude. Eventually, he was sure, it would work itself out.

The only trouble was that the hand did not get better. As the weeks on the line went by, it got so bad that when no one was looking he would whip off his thick cotton gloves and frantically massage the palm and fingers, pressing and pressing in an effort to relieve the agonizing throbs that were starting to travel all the way up his forearm when he clenched his file and set to work. It did not help.

After a while he began to think of the pain, as it burned its way through his hand, as a punishment and a trial, like the boils from which he had suffered without complaint during the last part of his hundred and seven days in the front lines. In his increasing loneliness, it became a companion to which he could talk silently. "Go away, you bastard," he would whisper to it; and if his attention were distracted, he would set to work and sometimes it really would go away. "Ah," he would say, "so I got rid of you that time."

But at night after he had fallen asleep all five fingers would stiffen like the legs of a crab, and they would remain that way until he had gotten into the car, driven to the factory, and begun to file, when they would gradually loosen up, only to be invaded by the returning pain. It became more and more difficult to conceal the stiffening from his wife, until one night, thrashing about in his sleep, he rolled over onto the tautened right hand and awoke with an irrepressible cry.

Wide-awake in an instant, as mothers are, Edith snapped on her lamp.

"Turn it off," he muttered. "It was me. I had a bad dream."

"Look at your hand," she said, sharp as a ferret. "What's wrong?"

"Nothing. It's just a little stiff. Turn off the light."

"A little stiff? It looks like a claw. Can I get you something? Does it hurt a lot?"

"Just sometimes," he replied, and could have kicked himself for his weakness. "Let's go to sleep, Edie. I'm tired."

"What do you mean, sometimes? How long has it been like that?"

"Off and on for a while." He turned over on his side, with his right arm hanging carefully over the edge of the bed, and closed his eyes.

"Go to see a doctor. Promise me you'll see a doctor."

"We'll see."

He had no intention of seeing a doctor even though, now that Edith knew about the fingers, which were beginning to snap back and forth uncontrollably, she began to nag him about it. For one thing, he saw no reason to go running for help just because she urged him to; for another, beyond all his pride in the record he was setting on the body-shop line was the fear that a doctor might do something to jeopardize it.

When he slashed his finger, though, catching his glove against the whirling edge of a grinding disc so that the cotton spun off and the disc bit into his flesh so viciously that blood spurted inside the torn glove all the way to the wrist, he had to go to the factory hospital. There the first-aid man wiped his hand clean and said, "Bend those fingers, will you, Mac, so I can make a neat bandage for you."

Wordlessly Orrin did as he was asked.

"Hey," the orderly said, "you got a trigger finger there, you know?"

"What's a trigger finger?"

"It clicks on you when you go to bend it, doesn't it, and then it won't come back by itself?"

"A couple of them are like that. It'll go away, won't it?"

"Can't prove it by me. You can soak it in the whirlpool, or better yet let the orthopedist see it — he comes in Wednesdays. Get a pass from your foreman next Wednesday for ten-thirty, okay?"

Orrin had no intention of seeing an orthopedist. But Edith saw the bandage and at once asked what they had said about his hand. When he told her, she was insistent that the practical thing to do was to cover himself against future disability and insure compensation by seeing the specialist.

Sheepishly, he asked Buster for a pass and walked on down to the hospital, past all those plant areas which seemed so soft and quiet, so clean and orderly, in comparison with the yelling, banging pressure of the body shop. It would be impossible for him, he thought, to stand around all day as these men did, clipping seat covers onto frames with small tools, spraying wheels with small guns as they swung silently by on overhead conveyers, or clamping cables onto batteries: this was woman's work, clean, dull, and deadly, and the men who did it looked incapable of getting down on their knees and working over a sheet of steel until the sweat streamed down and they remolded it to perfection. No wonder they earned less than he did — they were replaceable by anybody with two hands.

The orthopedist was a big bulky man in his forties, with a Masonic pin in the lapel of his tweed suit. He looked like a kindly former football player, and as Orrin extended his hand, palm up, for the examination, he knew that he would have to do what the doctor told him to — he felt, oddly, as though he were standing at attention before an officer about to give him orders. While the doctor poked and prodded gently, Orrin glanced at his own reflection in the gleaming chromium autoclave that stood against the tiled wall. He was astonished at how hangdog he looked, his bald forehead shining with the sweat of uneasiness, his body shrinking into the blue coveralls. My God, he thought, I look older than he does, and he turned his gaze hesitantly to the doctor's frank and friendly eyes.

"You've got a rare ailment," the doctor smiled, "known as tenosynovitis. Must be millions of people who have it."

"Is that what they call trigger finger?"

"The same. It's a callus growth around the sheath covering this tendon. The thicker it gets, the harder it is for the tendon to pull these fingers back and forth. In your case it'll probably become worse from the nature of your work, I regret to say."

"So there's nothing can be done?" Orrin asked, almost with relief.

"On the contrary, it's fairly easy to fix. Massage it with

cocoa butter from the second palmar crease toward this finger tip for a week. If that won't help, we'll open the hand and scrape away the callus. Sounds bad, but there's nothing much to it, and it always does the trick."

Orrin simply did not have time to sit around smearing grease into his hand which he used more than twelve hours a day; but he did it while he ate and during his relief time, for it seemed to him now that this slippery expedient was his last hope of avoiding the operation that represented in some indefinable way a threat to the continuity of his life.

It did not work. The orthopedist, in a dark blue suit this time, as befitted one pronouncing sentence, took up Orrin's hand with the same smiling gentleness and shook his head.

"Let's get it over with. The company will have you driven over to the hospital, so you name the day. I'm there every morning, operating, except Wednesdays and Sundays."

"Will I lose any time?"

The doctor put his thumbs in his vest, disclosing a row of cigars. "No reason why you should. You'll be a little groggy from the local for a while, but if you rest up for an hour I don't see why you can't come back here and finish up the day."

"It isn't the money." Orrin swallowed; the hand was burning. "It's just that . . . I can't hang around and not work."

"I think they'll give you something to do. The way our Social Security system operates, a big company finds it cheaper to have you come in with one hand than for you to sit home until it heals, collecting compensation for lost time. That sends up their insurance premiums, you see?"

The intricacies of such large-scale bookkeeping were beyond Orrin, but he felt somewhat relieved. He reported to the hospital in good time and was led to the operating room, where he lay staring up at the great round light overhead, silently proffering his right arm up to anesthetist, surgeon, and nurse, half dreaming of the day he had lain like this in the base hospital cursing with shame and weariness as they picked the shell fragments out of his legs and behind.

In an hour they had finished injecting, cutting, scraping, and sewing, and he arose swaying from the table, remembering fleetingly Edith and her narrow pelvis and the three girl babies she had borne, moaning and gritting her teeth, in this same building. Then he found himself in the company station wagon, blinking in the unaccustomed noonday light, and before he knew it he was back in the ambitious noise and dirt of the body shop.

He was greeted by Buster the foreman, who removed the cigar from his mouth, glanced appraisingly at the bandaged hand, and asked, "How'd it go?"

Orrin shrugged. He felt uneasy in his street clothes, without the coveralls, almost like one of the tourists who came through the plant in batches. "All right, I guess. It'll be all right. Got a job for me?"

"You can't metal-finish with all them stitches. You know there's no work on this line for one hand. Go on into the office and ask Hawks."

Hawks was the superintendent of the entire body shop; Orrin had spoken to him only two or three times. His office was in a glass and metal island in the middle of the area; it had five desks and telephones in as many cubicles for the engineers, inspectors, and technicians who drifted in and out. Waiting for Hawks, Orrin stood inconspicuously in a corner behind the glass with his arms clasped behind him, the good one supporting the throbbing one, watching the welders on the line before him, their cracking, sputtering guns strangely muted behind this thin glass barrier.

Hawks walked in swiftly and with a side glance at Orrin picked up a telephone from an empty desk and muttered something into it, then hung up. He was a tall, sagging man with a broken nose and pendulous earlobes. Every day he wore a freshly starched immaculate white shirt with the cuffs turned back, and an incongruously flashy tie secured by a silver clasp in the shape of a dollar sign. He was by gossip a woman chaser.

He said somberly, "What's up?"

Orrin extended his bandaged hand. "Buster said you could find a job for me. I just had this opened up this morning."

"God *damn* it. What do they think this is, a convalescent home?" He looked sadly at Orrin, as though he were pleading for understanding. *"You* know there's nothing in the body shop for a man with one hand. Sit down and take it easy, you must be still groggy. I'll see what I can do."

Orrin sat tensely on the edge of a metal chair, waiting for his new assignment. He had no idea what they would ask him to do. What he really wondered was how Buster and the rest were making out without him.

Hawks came back from one of the little cubicles where he had been muttering into a telephone. He hitched up his expensive slacks. "They need a man over in the chassis department. Go over to where they drive the cars off the line, on the way over to the hospital, and ask for Big Tony. He's a big dago, always has his hat on, always chews gum. Don't forget to give him your clock number, or you won't get paid."

Orrin made for the chassis department and introduced himself to Big Tony, who put down his clipboard and looked at him dubiously.

"Can you drive with one hand?"

"I can use the arm to steer."

"This kid's partner is out today. Take every other job as it gets to the end of the line. Don't forget they've never been driven, they're stiff — the eights should start, the sixes you got to choke. Watch for the automatic shift and the regular shift. There's only three places to take a job — over the pit for brake inspection, over onto that other line, or into the corner for repairs. I'll signal you which one to take. Go ahead, start this one up."

For Orrin it was exhilarating, bucking a line once again. The cars came off fast; sometimes he couldn't get them started, sometimes the automatic shift wouldn't work, sometimes there wasn't any seat inside and he had to steer from the floor, sometimes he drove into the wrong lane and had Big Tony howling curses at him. But it was good work for a one-armed man, and the time spun by so fast that he was astonished when the day was over.

"Boy, this was a tough one," sighed the youngster with whom he had been alternating jobs all day. "One of the toughest ever."

Orrin stared at him in disgust. The lad was no more than eighteen, myopic, with soft arms and a pimply forehead over his heavy eyeglasses. He said to him curiously, "How long have you been working here, anyway?"

"Two long months."

"Well, you ought to come on over to the body shop and find out what real work is like."

"No, thanks. I heard about it."

"This job was just right for me with one hand. If I had two hands, I'd fall asleep on it — and I'm practically twice your age."

Nevertheless, the following morning Orrin punched in quickly and hastened over to look up the boy. He saw him sitting by the huge air duct which sucked up the carbon monoxide as the cars came off the line.

"Okay, kid," he said. "I'm back to give you a hand again."

"Gee, I'm sorry," the boy replied, "but my partner's back today."

Orrin found himself waiting for an assignment once again on the edge of the metal chair in the body shop office. It was an hour and a half before Hawks came up and said absently, "See Buster. He'll give you something."

Until Hawks said these words Orrin had been shrinking down in the chair, avoiding the glances of the engineers and inspectors as they hurried in and out and mentally composing answers to some nonexistent executive who would come up to him and nudge him with his toe like someone tipping over a stone and say to him, *What are you doing for your pay, sitting there and staring off into space when everyone else in this plant is working like a dog?*

Now he arose, knowing that he had no answer, and walked slowly down the aisles to Buster, who stood at his desk painstakingly filling out requisition slips for tool repairs. Buster glanced up and said, "Oh, it's you," and at once led him away, as though afraid that Orrin would ask for permission to stay right there.

Orrin tagged after him silently, not walking alongside him so that Buster would feel that he had to make conversation. The foreman led him to a darkish corner at the rear end of the line at the beginning of the body shop, near the jigs where the bodies were first assembled, and indicated several barrels filled with small clips standing under a table.

"What you got to do is snap the green clips to the black

ones, like this. Make sure the narrow end is on top. Then take this can and brush and give them a smear, it's an oxide for rust. Can you do it one-handed?"

Orrin nodded wordlessly.

"Main thing is to keep ahead of that colored guy. He works here alone, mounts these to every job as you get them ready." He indicated a ghostlike Negro, humped and talking to himself at the far end of the line. Orrin reached out and touched Buster's arm.

"Who usually does this job?"

"Generally the colored guy does the whole thing himself. But they gave him one extra operation and it got to be too much. So I told Hawks and the time-study man to let you do this until they re-evaluate the job."

So he was being given made work. Leaning his hip against the work bench, Orrin watched, his insides quivering, as Buster without troubling to take the cigar from his mouth casually assembled a few of the license-plate clips and painted them as a kind of demonstration.

Controlling his voice, Orrin asked, "What about my relief?"

Buster smiled. "You won't kill yourself on this job. I can't spare the relief man for it. Take a twelve-minute break whenever you feel like it and you're far enough ahead. Take it easy, Orrin."

In the days that followed, Orrin learned what it meant to be stupefied. Mindlessly he snapped the little clips together, hundreds of them, thousands of them, his fingertips doing the childish little endlessly repeated trick while his mind was utterly free to roam as it pleased. For a while he amused himself as, he thought, any intelligent man would — by devising new and simpler ways to do the work, by laying out the clips in overlapping rows before beginning to snap them together, by spreading out the finished groups so that they could all be painted at once — but then there was nothing left for him to improve upon, the whole operation was basically stupid, and he fell back on allowing himself to get behind, dawdling along until the Negro assembler looked nervously at the dwindling pile of clips, and then working frenziedly to catch up. That was a game that could not be repeated indefinitely, though, and finally he simply slouched over the table, slipping the pieces together and dreaming — dreaming of the exalted moments of his past life, dwindled away now to little trinkets that had to be fitted together and smeared anyhow with paint.

He was home early evenings, since he could not work at the lumberyard, but if he could have thought of another place to go, he would have. Edith wanted to mother him and claimed it was nice to have him around for a change, and it drove him wild, as if he were already an old man finishing out his life as a night watchman, with a wife who plumped up his pillows and cut his corns for him.

"Can't you see I'm sick of it all?" he burst out one night. "If you hadn't been after me to do something about the hand, this would never have happened. I was working hard, pulling us out of the hole. I was the key man on the line, and now they've got me sorting nuts and bolts."

"I don't see what's so terrible if you take it easy for a while. You're still on the payroll. And you'll get back the money you're losing at the lumberyard in your workmen's compensation. Besides" — she looked at him narrowly — "you didn't want to stay on that assembly line forever, did you? I bet those other men you worked with would give anything to trade jobs with you right now."

That was the truth. But it didn't say much for the rest of the men. The next day he took a walk over to the line during his relief period, for the first time since he had been put in the corner with the Negro. Buster was standing there with his cigar in one hand and a soft cloth in the other, feeling the jobs as they went by and cursing out the men who had missed low spots. The line was moving fast, and everyone was working hard and steady; occasionally Walter or Pop the inspector or one of the others would look up and wave to him, but no one had time to come over and talk until Harold the pick-up man, his long, drunkard's nose twitching and his big Adam's apple bobbing like an alligator's snout, brushed up to him for a moment. Harold pointed with his buffer to a tall, tawny Negro with oriental eyes who was grinding away at a high spot, his long legs bent in a catcher's stance.

"That's your replacement," Harold said. "Not as good as you, but he knows his stuff. Life goes on, eh, Orrin? In point of fact, no matter what you do or how well you do it, there's always somebody around waiting to take over."

In a sudden rage, Orrin wanted to turn his back and walk away without any answer at all. But before he could move, Harold himself went back to the job, waving negligently at him as he left. Orrin stood for an instant, then walked over to Buster, now chewing his cigar like a cud and staring vacantly into space beyond the moving line.

"Hi, Buster," Orrin said. "Thought I'd come over during my break."

"How you making out over there, Orrin?" Buster asked incuriously.

"To tell you the truth, I'm going crazy. It's not for me. I was wondering if —"

"Excuse me," Buster muttered, and sprang forward to the bonderizing booth, where Hawks had turned up, alternately waving for Buster to hurry and arguing heatedly with Halstein, the chief inspector. Orrin turned and walked slowly down the aisles to his little corner, where the silent Negro was helping himself to a handful of painted clips.

"Fixing to do some myself if you didn't get back soon."

"Yes, well, that's all right," said Orrin absently. He made up a little batch for the man and then pulled back the bandage from his palm, peering into the dark area to see how the stitches were healing. It would have to be soon, he thought; if it didn't heal soon . . . If I was a kid, he thought, I'd run away from home.

The next morning, as he mooned over the little metal

snippets, remembering how Edith had once shown him the japanned box in which she kept all his V-mail from overseas, his commendation, and his ribbons, and wondering where that box was now, probably stuck away in a bottom drawer with a bunch of slips that needed mending, he was surprised to see Buster coming towards him with a young white-collar fellow in a brown gabardine suit, even balder than he was, whom he recognized as being from the payroll department.

"Fellow wants to talk to you for a minute, Orrin."

"I've got all day."

The payroll clerk laughed nervously. "If you remember last year, I came around to sign you up for your metal finisher's pay."

"I remember."

"I understand that since your injury and operation, you have been unable to perform metal finisher's work."

"Well, naturally . . . Say, wait a minute." Orrin flung aside the metal clips with which he had been toying. "Are you trying to tell me —"

"I'm only doing my job, fellow."

"Don't fellow me. You want to cut my pay, don't you? I ruin the damn hand metal-finishing and then you want to take away my metal finisher's pay. Well, you can take the stinking job and —"

"Take it easy, Orrin," Buster said uncomfortably. "It's nothing personal. This guy's got a job to do like anybody around here."

Orrin felt himself trembling from head to foot. "Is this the way they repay you for hard work? It's worse than the guards looking in your lunch box when you go out, to make sure you didn't steal five cents' worth of sandpaper. The hand's practically healed, I can go back to metal-finishing in a day or two, but that's not enough, is it? You got to take the lousy petty couple of dollars for these few days out of my hide. All right, take the money. And take the job too."

"It's got nothing to do with you or me. As soon as you go back on your old work, you go back on your old rate. You get paid for what you do — they can't make exceptions."

"I'm not talking about exceptions. I'm talking about whether a man is a human being or a piece of . . . My God," he cried out in anguish, "I might just as well have worked like all the others all year — nobody cares that I did my best."

Buster took him by the arm and led him away from the man in the brown suit. "Listen to me and don't be a jerk," he said intently. "You're not a kid to throw away a job just like that, you're a family man. Don't make a stink about the lousy five bucks, or whatever it is. They don't want to punish you for your operation, the place is too big, one hand doesn't know what the other one is doing. I wasn't supposed to tell you, but you're in line for a foreman's job on the night shift if you want. As soon as you get back on production again, Hawks is going to call you in." He nudged Orrin. "You know what I'm making, it's better than what you make. On salary, plus overtime, plus night-shift bonus, you'll do all right."

"Night shift," Orrin said slowly.

"They need bosses for nights. What do you care?" Buster added jocularly. "You're married a long time, you don't have to be home at night. You'll start fresh — new faces, you know? It's a break, Orrin. You don't want to be working all your life. I worked for sixteen years before they made me a boss."

Orrin thought of the living room where he hid from his wife behind the sports page of the paper at night; of the bedroom where she lay waiting for him when he worked alone in the lumberyard and came home late; of the half-finished children's room in the attic waiting for him to attack it once again, a final test of his fortitude. Then he looked at the bald-headed white-collar fellow as he stood waiting patiently with his ball-point pen and his little forms to be filled out, and he thought of the energy that he'd poured down the drain on job after job until now he was thirty-three and with nowhere to retreat beyond this ugly place where he had made his last-ditch resistance. Now he was being asked to sign his unconditional surrender.

He looked first at the payroll clerk, a little red in the face, then at Buster, holding a flaring lighter to his cigar stump, then at the solemn Negro, who had stopped work and was staring at the three of them, and he sighed.

"All right," he said at last. "Show me where to sign."

SIX

One for the Road

HAROLD'S hands were like the rest of him, long, bony, pale, and skillful. Except when he had a hang-over, they responded to every demand for swiftness and assurance. Now that he had gone on the wagon they were once again as supple and dextrous as they had been during his best days in the commercial-art field. The coarser work demanded by the auto-assembly line was more trying, but when they had hardened themselves to the sterner pressures of file and hammer they did not protest.

The rest of his body gave Harold somewhat more trouble. He was not used to standing on his feet for long hours without leaning on a bottle, and his thighs, his back, and the soles of his feet protested bitterly during his first few weeks on the line in the body shop. He was a man of thirty-nine, accustomed to sitting hunched over a drawing board, accustomed, too, to being primed with liquor even before brushing his teeth, but he was willing to bear this new misery patiently. It semed reasonable to hope that it would pass more quickly than other miseries he'd had in his time.

"Aches and pains are nothing," he said to Buster, his foreman, with whom he had gotten along well from their very first meeting. "You can always buy a bottle of liniment. It's the heartache that you have to watch out for. I've swallowed a lot of internal medicine for that, and it never did me a bit of good."

Buster had taken a liking to Harold at once. He had never had occasion to talk with a professional artist, and he was plainly impressed. Besides, although his own brother-in-law was practically a rumhead, he had never before met anyone who frankly said of himself, as Harold did, "I'm an alcoholic."

Harold knew that the foreman's friendliness mixed snobbery and curiosity, but he had no objection as long as it made Buster go a little easier on him. The desire to be friendly with someone whose background you associated with prestige and good living was only human. As for the nosiness, there couldn't have been any if Harold himself hadn't come out and said he was a drunk.

That was one of the few things, he thought wryly as he ground away at the job before him, that no one had explained to this drunkard working at becoming an ex-drunkard. All the doctors and the A.A. boys were ready with one explanation after another of the drinking compulsion; but none of them had come up with an explanation of the damned compulsion to talk about it once you had quit, except that it was supposed to be part of the therapy to share your story.

Soon after Harold's probationary period was up, Buster said, "I want you to go on pick-up today, chief. If you want extra overtime, this is your chance. It's always the pick-up men that get asked first to stay on to clean up the dead-line, and sometimes to metal-finish over in final paint."

"Thank you, boss. I appreciate it."

"You've been doing good work. And I know you're one of the few that never turns down overtime. Besides," he added in a burst of candor, "some guys just won't stay on pick-up. All that grinding, they're afraid of the lead getting in their lungs."

"I've put worse things in my insides in my time," replied Harold. "I'll take my chances with the lead if I can have the overtime."

"Here, start on this job. On pick-up you haven't got time to do much filing, unless the supervisor or the inspectors make you. You're responsible for a smooth finish on all the lead that's been flowed on, so grind around these edges of all the station wagons, just underneath where the chrome trim goes. I'll show you the rest as you go along."

Harold was bluntly and unashamedly anxious for the overtime. The money part he didn't have to speak of. The other part he had no hesitation in explaining.

"The longer I work on the line," he said, not only to

Buster but to the other pick-up men and to Pop the inspector, "the more I knock myself out, the less chance there is of my falling off the wagon. I might as well get paid for taking the treatment."

Perhaps there was an element of self-pity in his explanation, of appealing to the others for sympathy. Harold thought of that, but it didn't interest him much one way or the other. He didn't feel like an object of pity, not now that he was making his own way, and he worked sixty and seventy hours a week the way other men work forty. Once the line had stopped, after eight or nine or sometimes ten hours, it made no difference what they gave him to do; he felt that he was coasting, and his weariness wore off as the eleventh and even the twelfth hour wore by. One day it would be the dead-line, that long row of rejected bodies next to the bonderizing booth which had to be repaired to pass inspection; another day it would be similarly rejected cars which had already been completely assembled and painted. In either case Harold was content to stay on. With the jobs standing still and obediently waiting for him to finish them to perfection, there was no pressure on him, and he was free to taper off from the steady grind of meeting every other job as it moved up to him on the platform at the end of the assembly line. Besides, he was free to daydream.

The truth was that once his body had stopped complaining the automobile factory had no physical reality for Harold. This he dared not explain to anyone; he sensed that it was far more dangerous than confessing that you were a lush, because it called into question your attitude not just toward yourself but toward those with whom you shared this state of suspended being. Nevertheless it was so. Harold — who knew himself as a tall, sallow, Adam's-appled, pompadoured, stoop-shouldered commercial artist and a quart-and-a-pint-a-day man — felt that he had no present, that he hung suspended between past and future, both of which grew more vivid as his sense of present reality receded eerily into infinity like the girl in the di Chirico painting rolling a hoop into nothingness.

The present had no texture for him partly by contrast with the richly pain-laden past, much of which he was able to describe aloud with the flat jocularity of a travel guide, inserting a little joke now and then to liven up the historical stretches. Harold knew that it was possible for him to express his feelings about the past to the men on the line only because the men partook of the present's unreality, and could not color the black-and-white picture he drew for them. They were simply receptacles for his recapitulation of how it had come about that he, a city boy, a night bird, a good letterer and better poster man, found himself in this unlikely sunlit nightmare.

At that, there were things he couldn't tell them, memories floating up to consciousness in the wake of other flotsam that he dredged up for their delectation.

"How'd you get started drinking, Harold?" the foreman worked up the courage to ask. This was after Harold had stated that his liquor bills, even when he was working steady and only drinking the way other people chewed gum, had run to eight bucks a day.

"Been drinking ever since I can remember," Harold replied. "In point of fact, bootleg booze was always around the house. I can recall being drunk when I was six or seven years old, from sampling leftovers."

"But how come your folks let you drink?"

"There was just my father. He was a hard drinker himself, and he couldn't keep his eye on me. By the time I was in high school I always had a pint in my locker. I was tough. The other kids used to whisper about me."

This was impressive, shocking even, for the men on the line. But they had no way of knowing how it had been in fine detail. They couldn't know without his telling them, which he didn't, that since Harold's father had been accountant for a paper-cup company, his house had always been one vast litter of paper cups. Harold's earliest memory was of crawling around on the parlor floor pushing a train made of the long cardboard cartons that the cups came in; and later of stringing the stark-white cones into necklaces and festoons which lay around gathering dust, waiting for the occasional cleaning woman to sweep them into the garbage can. He could not have been very long out of kindergarten when he discovered that many of the flat-bottomed kind, the ones his father left standing around on dressers and end tables, had a few drops of burning liquid in them.

Harold grew to learn that the drinks his father left lying around helped put him to sleep when he lay alone in his "youth bed" waiting in vain for someone to tuck him in. Often, very often, there were strange women who came in after dinner and danced to the Atwater Kent console until Harold's bedtime. Then while he lay in bed hugging his koala bear, they would really begin to carouse — Harold's father and his woman of the evening — howling, cursing, breaking glass despite the abundance of paper cups. Sometimes they would still be there in the morning when he padded past his father's door in his Doctor Dentons.

As he grew older, he would lie in bed with the bootleg whisky in the paper cups, envying not his burly, roaring father, who seemed never to want for the company of passionate and loving women, but the women themselves for the exclusive attention they received from Daddy. But in reality there could not have been so very many evenings when he lay huddled in bed drinking the corn he had learned to dilute with water and wishing he were the roistering woman locked in with his father.

Actually, this was all a little too clinical. In retrospect, Harold was inclined to suspect that the reasons for his drinking were both deeper and shallower. In either case, they were less spectacular. He had always been agonizingly shy as a kid, and the little things that heightened his feelings of inadequacy and aloneness were so little that they hardly seemed worth building into salesworthy reminiscence: the only kid in the class who had nobody come to Open House, even though his father had done him a favor and joined the P.T.A.; the kid who always ate lunch alone in the school basement because the housekeepers who made his half-hearted peanut-butter sandwiches never thought to insert any tradable home-baked cookies; the kid who never dated in high school but had the nerve — after a quick snifter from the bottle stashed in his locker — to tell the vice-principal to go screw in front of everybody . . . Anyway, liquor had been the Great Lubricator for him.

But Buster, intent on condemning the monster who could carelessly poison an only son, said to him one day, "I've been thinking about that father of yours. I hope you don't mind my saying so, but he must have been one son of a bitch."

"Oh, he was." Harold nodded his head judiciously. "Still . . . he managed to hold down his job all those years. In point of fact, he was an officer of the company toward the end. He was at a sales conference at the Hotel Pontiac in Buffalo when he died of apoplexy. Actually, he was in the sack with a floozy, celebrating Repeal. I was seventeen."

Buster shook his head sadly. "No wonder you took to drink."

"Oh, but I'll tell you something. He surprised me. I mean after he died. He left me ten thousand bucks in cold cash, and he had it tied up so that I could only use it to go to school — so much a year, and I had to get passing marks. So he guaranteed my college education that way. Now you wouldn't expect that of a man like him, would you?"

Buster was more impressed with the revelation that Harold was indeed a college man. He would have found it hard to understand that, given the great opportunity, Harold had muffed it. He had majored in art, and he had gotten the grades necessary for his allowance, but he had been lonely and miserable, convinced after a while that he was headed noplace in the fine-arts world and that he was never going to be popular as a person. He got on best at college with the heavy drinkers; but they were a very social lot, and in their company — particularly when they started making vacation plans together — Harold felt very much the lonely orphan.

Two years after graduation he had been through four jobs and he needed at least a pint to get through the day, not counting the quick ones whenever he passed a bar. It was at an Eighth Street bar that he met Marie one tuberculous winter's night.

He had just been fired from the fourth job and was well on the way to tying one on when Marie, a thin blond Jewess in rayon slacks, touched him on the arm and asked him why he was unhappy. It was the sort of thing that could happen in the Village, before the war.

Six weeks later they were married, because he was terrified of losing her and because Marie felt it would hurt her parents less if she brought home as a husband a pale, underfed Gentile with a big Adam's apple than if they were to discover that she had been living in sin. She and Harold had two years together before Pearl Harbor, and then she followed him from one camp to another until he was shipped out.

Three different men on the line asked: "Did she know you drank when she married you?"

"That was how we met," he would reply, showing his long, discolored teeth. "I often thought she married me *because* I drank. It gave her a chance to mother me."

And it gave her somebody to feel superior to, he thought; she was smart enough to latch on to somebody in worse shape than she was. Or was he only trying to evade his guilt at what he had done to the only person who had ever really loved him by stepping on her memory with his heel as he stepped on his own?

Once he was thousands of miles from home he had virtually quit drinking. It wasn't, oddly enough, until he was being rotated back home from the Islands that he had gone on a terrible bat aboard the troop transport. Shy as he was, and sly as he was, he'd sweet-talked the denatured alcohol out of the ship's carpenter and jimmied the grapefruit juice from the locked galley, and then set up a still. The other heroes had been lucky enough to vomit their insides out, but he had had the lion's share and as a result was stone-blind for the last two weeks of the voyage. He had gotten his sight back just two days before docking.

When he and Marie finally fell into each other's unfamiliar arms, each wept at the other's pallor and thin strangeness after the three lost years. They returned to Marie's Village apartment and to the teaching job she had gotten when it became clear that her sculpture would not go. There came a time, all too soon, when Harold couldn't hang around the female place alone while she was back at her blackboard; but remembering with terror the blindness, he dared not pull up a stool at the corner tavern.

"My wife made a thing out of letting me get to be a civilian again," Harold said affectionately. "The longer I took to do it, the more casual she got about it. She must have read someplace that that was the way to handle the problem. Maybe she wrote a letter to Dorothy Dix."

"But the drinking . . ."

"In point of fact, Buster," Harold replied, "I got to feel after a while that I'd be doing Marie a favor if I went out and tied one on. She was silently begging for the opportunity to nurse me. Didn't she deserve a better reason for feeling superior than just that she was working and hubby wasn't?"

Buster was bemused by this, and Harold was led to consider just how much of what he had been confiding in the foreman was true, anyway, and how much was a kind of inverse bragging. Am I still taking everything out on Marie, he wondered, after all these years? Am I still flogging her for being patient with me and kind to me, instead of . . . of what? What else did I want of her?

Nevertheless it was true that he had gone back to the old medicine to keep his upper lip stiff and that its immediate effect had been to give Marie a good workable explanation of why his reconversion was being delayed. They'd shuffled along like that for a while, with him barging in stinko from the jobs he held for a week or a month, yelling back at the neighbors who pounded on the pipes, and yielding while Marie ice-bagged and prune-juiced him back into shape. But it got worse, as it had to, and chasms began to yawn: she wanted a baby, and she wasn't getting any younger; and when was he going to start taking some of the load off her back; and wasn't it time that he discovered that there was more to life than bottle parties, nausea, and amnesia.

What happened was that he discovered something else. He discovered that he was not merely a hard drinker, but a drunk. For a time he took a vicious satisfaction in believing that the final shove overboard had been Marie's crying the blues about babies (the very thought panicked him) and jobs (each was stupider than the preceding one, and boredom set in increasingly fast when he parked his fanny before a drawing board), and that if she hadn't started to play wifey in such frightening earnest he might have gone on handling the stuff as he had been able to more or less before the war; but after a while, when he was on a sustaining program of a quart and a pint a day, none of the reasons for it seemed to matter much any more.

They shot from one gruesome episode to another, like two characters in a comic strip that he was drawing bam-sock-zowie for posterity instead of for money. Good and loaded, he had told off the Brooklyn in-laws during what he hadn't even known were the High Holidays, and Marie's brothers had thrown him bodily out of the old folks' apartment on Eastern Parkway. Bad and loaded, he had encoun-

tered the advertising agency art director who was his cur-
rent boss munching shrimp with his mistress at a flossy
sidewalk restaurant, had swiped a shrimp from the bulbous
mistress's plate, and wound up — one remark leading to
another and the fancy lady flouncing furiously from the
table — being boosted past the curb by the headwaiter and
two bellboys, with Marie desperately and hopelessly trying
to quiet him, free him from the hotel stooges, and com-
mandeer a cab. As a last straw, when she had found him
well-stiffed in a quiet bar, he had street-fought his sobbing
wife up and down Lexington Avenue in broad daylight,
yelling after her things about the Jews that had never occurred to him before but that he knew would hurt her more
than a black-and-blue beating.

That did it. Marie got a new lock for the door and he
went out like a light. When he came to four days later in a
mission on West Forty-second around Tenth Avenue, he
found purple bruises in unmentionable places on his body.
The left hip pocket, the one in which he kept his wallet, had
been cut out of his pants with a razor blade.

The fine points of all this, the detailed itinerary of his
odyssey, so to speak, he did not touch on when he recounted his past to his foreman and to the one or two others
on the line who served as the recipients of these confi-
dences. Harold did not feel that he was holding back unfairly; on the contrary, he was proud of his ability to strip
the past and serve its bare bones objectively. He tended
sometimes to repeat himself and sometimes to foul up the

chronology, but by and large he gave his working companions what sounded like an honest outline.

"I was willing to concede that I was a drunk," he told them, "but I was damned if I'd admit that I was nothing more than a bum. After Marie threw me out, it began to look as though I couldn't be one without being the other. That was what scared me, more than the idea that I was tied to the booze like a kid to a balloon. I was drinking over on the East Side by then because they knew me in the Village and didn't want any part of me, and finally I got right into the gutter with the winos down on the corner of Canal and the Bowery, waiting with a dust rag for the light to turn red to wipe your windshield and bum a dime toward a bottle of sherry or the price of a flop."

Never mind that he hadn't actually done that. He *had* panhandled for the first and last time over on Cortlandt Street, where there was small likelihood of being recognized, and had promptly bumped by agonizing chance into an acquaintance named Schwartz, not rich, not kind, just a middle-aging Gold Star father who owned a letter shop, had five employees, and kept his dead son's tinted photo on his desk. Schwartz wouldn't let him crawl away, pulled him into one of those White Rose taverns where bums and businessmen mingle over pastrami and knackwurst, and with nobody paying any attention bought them a couple of beers. Then he gave him twenty-five and told him to get the hell out of town, told him to get a factory job at the new auto plant and wear himself out working for a while.

"Well, gents, I've been here now exactly two hundred and fifty-three days, not counting a little siege of grippe, and I haven't had one drink in all that time. Paid my rent, bought a car — first one I ever owned — and even put away a little something. Came here out of curiosity and used it up in a hurry, but in point of fact how could I say I'm sorry?"

This was bringing him perilously close to the present, and there were only one or two other questions that he could answer. Such as:

"Did you finally get divorced?"

"Oh no, no." He kept it casual. "I'll be seeing Marie again one of these days." This telescoped the whole period, starting from the time he had written Marie giving her his new address, with no answer; to the time he had written her that he had been working on the line for eighty-seven days without a drink, with no answer; for a hundred and ninety-four days without a drink but with plenty of overtime and double features on restless nights, with no answer. After nine months he had written:

DEAR MARIE,

I hope the reason you haven't been answering is that you've been waiting to see does he mean business. I think 270 days of gruelling hard work and NO DRINKS is business and I am praying that you will answer now. There was no sense before in my saying I was sorry. You wouldn't have believed me and I had no way to prove it to you. But I hope you believe me now, since you always used to say

*Actions speak louder etc. I'm NOT appealing to your pity.
I'm not even asking to come back on the old terms because
it wouldn't do either of us any good. But I have to have
something to look forward to if I am going to finish my
comeback. So would you just write and say you're all right.
Just let me start to look ahead instead of rehashing the past
and I know you will find that I am a different person. Don't
let me down.*

HAROLD

That one she had answered:

DEAR HAROLD,

*Frankly, I didn't think after all these years you'd have
the guts to do what you are doing. I haven't answered because I thought if I did you'd come back here and the whole
business would only start all over again. But I am keeping
my fingers crossed for you, and from now on I promise to
answer your letters promptly.*

YOUR WIFE

*P.S. School is the same. Since I have all my evenings
free I have gone into leather work. It is much more satisfying now than working with stone. Less surprises, but
you're sure it will turn out worth while. M.*

So now here he was. It was true at last that he was corre-
sponding with his wife, now that he had no more debt to
Schwartz (at least no more money debt), a paid-up car, a
bank account, and a dry palate. Once he had brought himself up to date there was simply nothing more he could add
to his summation of the past without unfairly revealing the

unreality of the present or exposing the delicate shape of the future, of which he was now free to daydream constantly.

He had made a funny pen-and-ink sketch of himself banging out dents in the body shop which he had rolled into a tube and sent to Marie, figuring shrewdly that it would mean more to her than a wedding anniversary present chosen from an arty gift shoppe. From her he had received a calfskin wallet, cut and sewed by hand and tooled at the corners with private symbols which no one else could have recognized, recalling better days. *This is to hold all that money you're saving,* she had written, and after that he had written to ask when he could come to see her.

For now he had achieved every limited goal he had set himself but that of reunion with his wife. He was perfectly convinced at last that alcohol was a poison for him. He had certainly reached a point of distance from which he could speak of his past frankly to people like Buster, who were friendly but really meant nothing to him. And most important of all he had proved to himself and now to Marie that he could last out a life which was so regular, so routinized, so howlingly dull that it made his previous commercial art jobs seem like skin diving for sunken Phoenician barges off the Riviera dei Fiori.

I have done it, he wrote to Marie, and I am doing it. In the evenings I go to the movies, one after another. In the daytime I punch in and I punch out, and in between without any liquid stimulation whatsoever I am the perfect mechanical man, well liked by one and all and even good at what I do. Whoever would have guessed it? And Marie was answering (for he had attained the fourth of his five goals, that of re-establishing contact with his wife) with increasing enthusiasm and pride in his comeback from alcoholism to anonymity, dropping little hints here and there, not unlike the newspaper filler items about yak production in Tibet or decreases in the disease rate of Uruguayan sheep, that an artist with a clear eye and a steady hand would have exciting opportunities in the television world.

Of course there was a catch to it all. There had to be, just as there always was when an elderly bookkeeper won a walking race, or a suburban mother of three won a trip around the world by correctly answering pathological questions about tropical diseases. In Harold's case the trick of keeping his equilibrium on the line (sometimes he thought of himself as a tightrope walker who had conquered hereditary vertigo) was in accepting the unreality of the present and forging — now that he had bared the past to his fellow wraiths — a chain of the most delectable daydreams. The dreams, for all their insubstantiality and vagueness, were so sunny and delightful that, just as he used to wait impatiently for the liquor store to open, so now he could hardly wait for morning, to begin grinding and filing and buffing, and then gradually to immerse himself in the warm bath of the future, released at last from bondage to bottle or machine.

Marie did her bit all unknowingly — or did she know? —

by dangling before him the prospect of money, success, and the penitence of those who had once wronged him by doubting his core of sobriety and his essential ability. She would not, in response to his pleas, tell him when he should come, or even set some arbitrary deadline after which he could return in triumph. Instead, egged on, Harold suspected in those moments of black doubt that still assailed him, by a psychologist whom she consulted for a fee, she wrote that she was going to leave the date and circumstances of their eventual reunion to Harold's own considered judgment, and that this indeed was to be his final step in the achievement of self-mastery.

So Harold, free to dream, fantasied everything — the works, the whole game — at least, up to a point. Bankbook in hand, he tapped the horn lightly before the gaping apartment house, and Marie, thinner, yes, but wide-eyed at his natty smile and his Simonized automobile, came running out to take him by an arm more heavily-muscled than she had ever known it.

After that the daydream stubbornly refused to proceed. Refractory as a torn strip of film which stops feeding itself through the machine just as the romance is at its most tantalizing and flashes off instead the upside-down reel numbers before blacking out completely, his dream refused to budge further. Its recalcitrance was not maddening to Harold, only puzzling, and therefore challenging. He was perfectly content to start up the dream over and over, if only because it felt so good; and after a few days the question What comes next? was resolved in fantasy only in a generalized glow of sunny prosperity and mutually loving contentment for himself and Marie, a hazy but voluptuous aura without source and without end. It was so good that Harold could stop thinking of it at any point and go off to lunch, to the toilet, or to a particularly difficult job with two inspectors and an engineer hanging over him and then return to it without skipping a beat.

Nevertheless, only Marie's letters and his bankbook linked the actual present to any realizable future. Harold's exuberance over his steadily mounting savings was tempered by an uncomfortable awareness — despite Marie's delicacy in never once referring to it — that he had never sent her so much as a dime from the day all this had started. Still, he had it now, cash that he just hadn't had in all the mottled and blotched years since the war. One Saturday morning, standing at the teller's window, he stared at the new entry stamped in the little book, and then he looked up in triumph and smiled into the startled teller's number-bound eyes. I am ready, he said to himself.

He hastened back to his room to compose a letter to Marie, advising her that if it was all right with her he would work through the coming week and would leave for the city directly after work on Friday, stopping only for a quick bite.

Her reply was waiting for him on Tuesday evening when he arrived at the rooming house, weary and needing a bath. The envelope stood on end on top of *Life* magazine, propped against the discolored brass lamp on the hall table. His heart was pounding fast, and as he reached out for the letter with the familiar handwriting, he had the feeling that there was a hand inside the envelope reaching out for his too.

All day Wednesday he could not make up his mind whether to announce to the men on the line that he was driving down to see his wife on Friday night. It would be a violation of his principle never to talk of the future; on the other hand, it seemed to him now that only cowardice could possibly keep him from mentioning something as ordinary as what he planned.

That night he could not sleep, and it was raining too hard for a trip to the movies. He heard the television going down in the parlor; he tucked his shirt into his pants, letting the belt out a notch (how he'd fattened since going on the wagon!), and pattered downstairs in his slippers to join the landlady on the sofa. He watched her screen until his eyes crossed, captured more by the commercials than by the programs they paid for. For a man of his taste and his talents, there was more imaginative appeal in the commercials than in the entertainment they surrounded. But then, thinking of what Marie had already written about commercial-art possibilities in television and of what he would have to do if he were to make his daydreams come true, he began to grow anxious. To his intense annoyance, he discovered that his palms were starting to sweat; he excused himself and went to bed.

First thing next morning he slipped in a casual remark that Friday evening he'd be off to see his wife. The revelation aroused no more curiosity than if he had announced his intention to go to a night ball game. Orrin was going to spend the week end at his lumberyard job and his house remodeling; Benny, the colored pick-up man, had a job driving a truck; Tommy, who went to night school, had exams to bone up on; the new man, a recently returned old-timer named Frank, was going to the trotters Friday night. Harold was chagrined when he saw that his news was scarcely commented on.

He said nothing more about it. But on Friday he arose before dawn to get his things together, shave, and bathe. He wore his good clothes to work and changed into his usual gray cotton shirt and trousers in the locker room. Something told him that it would be better to go straight to Marie from the factory; maybe it was the half-conscious fear that if he went back to the rooming house he might find a last-minute change of mind propped against the lamp on the hall table.

Buster rotated his cigar and eyed him nonchalantly. "Want some overtime today, Harold? Going to be a couple hours' work on the dead-line."

"No, thanks." It was the first time he had ever declined. "Going to New York as soon as we knock off. Have to meet my wife."

"Oh, that's right," Buster said. "You told me, I forgot. So

I guess you won't want to work tomorrow if we get the call."

Harold shook his head and glanced at his watch. "Not this week end."

He fought off a strong, irrational desire to pull back the cuff of his glove and sneak another look at the watch he had just examined. Filing furiously, working harder than he had in a long time in order to speed the hour, he wondered if the others on the line would be so calm if they had what he had to look forward to. He had arranged his schedule with the relief man so that his break came almost at the end of the shift — it would enable him to hurry off scrubbed and clean, but it also made the day longer. At last the relief man showed up and said, "Take twelve minutes, Harold," and he made for the bathroom.

He lathered up well, turning his wiry, hairless arms carefully to make sure that the dirt above and behind the elbows was gone, and he soaked his hair too, so that it would comb easily. As rigid as an actor awaiting his on-stage cue on opening night, he inspected his farmer's Adam's apple in the mirror for spots maybe missed with the razor at dawn, and brought his wet, stiff rows of hair into a tall, sliding pompadour.

When the siren blew, he punched out silently. As he was dropping his time card into the rack, Frank, the new old-timer, clapped him on the back and said in his bluff, loud voice, "See you Monday, right?"

"Don't be too sure," Harold replied over his shoulder, and went off hurriedly to avoid questions. But it was so: who could predict the future? Maybe he would be coming back just to collect his final pay and say goodby to those who were stuck on the line. It was most probable, and it awed him. Why had he never felt this way before about all his other jobs? He found himself touching familiar objects in an almost superstitious farewell — stacks of batteries, painted fenders swinging from hooks, glossy mufflers — as he made his way to the exit gate.

He drove his old car up to the diner which stood on a bluff across the highway from the plant and took a place in an empty booth near the door, facing the TV screen. It was a combination bar and restaurant and was already filled with day men who had hurried in for a quick one on the way home to more sober affairs, and with night men too, somewhat more quietly sipping coffee before going to work.

"Will a steak take long?" Harold asked the waitress.

"You'll have it before you know it."

"I don't want it that fast. In point of fact, I want to look forward to it, medium rare. Coffee with it, and some tomato juice first."

While he sipped his juice, someone was flirting with the TV dial. The ball game had just ended and the search for something else had begun. At last they settled for a row of marching cigarettes; the cigarettes went forward, stumbled, diminished, multiplied, pullulated, singing as they went. The screen was full of them, thousands of them, and their piping voices grew louder and louder. Harold pulled out a pack of cigarettes, cursing himself for his susceptibility. His fingers were shaking so that he could hardly get one free of the pack.

It was just that it raised the question of whether the rainbow road to those daydreams was lined with marching cigarettes, and whether at age forty he could catch on as an animator or as whatever else you had to be to make it go nowadays.

Letting the smoke simmer through his nostrils, Harold turned deliberately from the screen and gazed out the steamy window at the smooth, modern bulk of the factory glowing incandescently a quarter of a mile away. It looked like nothing so much as a splendid, progressive new prison, conceived and executed by an architect who knew how to use glass and aluminum to conceal concrete pillboxes and whirling searchlights; at this moment he would not have been at all surprised to hear the wail of a siren announcing his escape. How did I stick it out so long, he marveled, how did I keep from going stir-crazy?

The answer was almost dreadfully clear. He knew it as soon as he admitted to himself that he was afraid to leave the factory, afraid to exchange its impersonal, endless subjection for the ministrations of the kindly keeper who waited for him with love and patience. On the line nothing was demanded of him beyond what you would ask of a bullock, or an intelligent slave. That was all he needed to keep him sober. But now that he was leaving, he sensed

with a chattering terror the demands that would be made
on his poor wits when he would be expected to live by
them and not by his brawn; when he would be expected (if
only by himself) to act like a man, and not like a bullock
or a slave — or a drunk; and he knew why it was that he
used Marie — who loved him compassionately, as no one
ever had before or would again — as a kind of city dump for
everything that he feared and hated about his own aging
self. She wanted him to be a free and independent man at
last, with his own identity, but it could not be done unless
she encircled him as a wedding ring encircles a finger. Was
it a hopeless paradox?

Directly beneath his window, so close that he could practically jump down onto it if the window were open, like a
cowboy making his getaway, stood his old coupe, curried,
combed, and snaffled for New York and Marie. Slowly he
traced the number 40 on the steamed glass with his index
finger, then rubbed it out. Through the cleared circle
his car was zeroed in as if in a bull's-eye, its nose pointing
toward his destination.

The cigarettes had turned to snowflakes — magnified
crystals like illustrations from the *Book of Knowledge* —
through which a man and a woman were skating with
crossed hands, singing cheerily of the washing wonders
worked by soapflakes. Then the steak was before him, long,
fat, and greasy on the heavy china platter. As he peered
down at the globules of blood and fat skimming slowly
like skaters over the nothingness of the gravy, Harold's

gorge rose. You'll have to get it down, he told himself grimly, you'll have to get it down.

But how will I pay? He patted his left hip (no more razored-out pockets) to ascertain whether the wallet Marie had sent him was in these trousers or out in the car. Yes, there it was. He pulled it out and glanced within: plenty.

For the first time he felt a stiffness in one of the compartments. Curiously he worked his long, narrow finger inside and withdrew a small pasteboard. It was a plain blue-and-white identification card, just what you usually find in new wallets.

But Marie had made the wallet by hand. Why should she have put such a card inside? Had she gone to the trouble just as a jocular reminder that the wallet wasn't really machine-made? Or . . . or what?

Harold peered at it a little more closely. There were spaces for his name, his address, his blood type. Then it said: *In Case of Accident Please Notify . . .*

The card was trembling in his fingers. Furious with himself, he pushed away the steak platter and set down the card in its place, then reached into his jacket pocket for his fountain pen. As he was uncapping it, the waitress came back to his booth and said in a friendly fashion, "You ought to eat your steak first. It's no good cold."

With a start, Harold nodded. "I will. Listen, bring me a double whisky, will you?"

The plump, plain girl looked at him in surprise. "Say, I never saw you drink before. Not even beer."

"You're so right. I don't drink. But I've got a hard ride before I get back to the ranch. I may need one for the road."

When she returned with the whisky glass and a little scalloped paper napkin and a larger glass with ice water and swizzle stick, she demanded, "Mix it?"

Harold shook his head.

"Listen," she said nervously, "I know it's none of my business, but maybe you shouldn't —"

"Ah," he broke in, "word gets around, doesn't it? I'll tell you what. You just put it right down here, next to this little card. And I'll just sit here for a while and think about whether or not."

When she had done that, Harold picked up the fountain pen once again and began to cap and uncap it, cap and uncap it, waiting for the girl to go away and for the terrible deadly pangs in his insides to come to a tidal climax.

SEVEN

Just One of the Boys

LOOKING back on twenty-five years of factory life, Buster felt reasonably proud that he had always supported his wife and daughter decently, and had worked up to becoming a foreman without acquiring the reputation of being either a climber or a schemer. He emphasized the soberness of his North German face in one way with a cigar, in another with the heavy-lensed eyeglasses that his increasing nearsightedness forced on him. When he thought how his once powerful father, crippled in an industrial accident, had wasted away uselessly in a wheel chair, a burden instead of a provider to his wife and children, Buster was inclined not so much to complain about having had to go to work at fourteen, as to be pleased with what he had achieved as an uneducated man.

Buster had stuck it out on the auto assembly line as a

spot welder for sixteen years, through the depression and most of the war; and when he put away his staff sergeant's uniform and came home from Louisiana, he claimed his seniority, no longer with any great expectations but feeling that it was only prudent, especially with rising expenses and a daughter starting school. Within a year he became a foreman; from time to time he was shifted from one line to another, but always it was made clear that his good qualities were appreciated, and there were even hints of better things to come.

Buster liked being a boss. "Never mind that I wear clean clothes now," he said to his wife one day. He held out his heavy hands to her across the kitchen table. "I worked for a long time and I'm willing to work again if I have to. What feels good is that I'm handling sixteen men because the company knows I know how to handle men. Not because I'm harder than the next man, or because I was against the union in the old days, or sucked around the bosses. The company knows where I stand and the men know where I stand." He could not keep from adding, "There's not many foremen can say that."

"I know, Carl," his wife replied. Her mind was on the hem of her daughter's dress that she was taking up. Lines were encircling Agnes's throat like necklaces and embedding themselves forever, and the truth was that she did not want him to be too satisfied. Before it was too late, she wanted him to move up again.

Buster was willing to make the effort, just as he was willing to recognize that the little things that went with being a boss gave him as much pleasure as his improved status gave his wife. After nine years of it, he still liked coming to work in a dirty place with clean clothes on and knowing that he was not going to get them dirty. And everything that went with clean clothes. Not having to punch a time clock, but dropping in early instead to the body shop office to sign in and sit around on a desk edge talking over production problems. Not having to eat out of a lunch box on the floor, or in the huge, prisonlike cafeteria with its long tables sprayed with spat-out grape pits, tipped-over sugar bowls, wet bread crusts expanding in pools of coffee, and cigarette butts put out in Jello, but at one of the quiet, clean tables in the supervisors' wing of the cafeteria. Not having to change into overalls in the vaulted locker rooms smelling of tired men and tired feet, but hanging his hat and sport jacket in the foremen's private locker room.

And of course the money. Just as it was better to be the man who handed out the sixteen pay checks than to be one of the sixteen who received them, it was better to know that the check given you privately was a salary, plus overtime that added up to a decent living.

Naturally you paid a penalty. You were constantly nagged by every boss who stood above you; there was no recourse if they chose to knife you, and if you wanted the job bad enough you held still and let them stick it into you. But to Buster this was the way life was; and if you were any good at handling sixteen workers, you ought to be pretty fair at

handling sixteen bosses. After all these years the top brass
knew him as well as they knew anyone at his level, and
they didn't often chew him out as long as he pulled production on his line.

But then the company built an enormous new plant out
in the sticks, and after the big move Buster found that his
problems were not only multiplied but infinitely more complicated than he had ever thought possible. In the old factory they had been building cars for over a quarter of a
century. Everyone knew where everything was; everybody
knew everybody else — almost, anyway.

Here, however, there was a solid year of trial and error,
of sweating and cursing and hiring and firing, of breakdown
and repair, and even then production was not what it
should have been; even then the big wheels rolled in from
Michigan and struck terror into the heart of every boss in
the building.

The basic trouble, as Buster was not alone in seeing, was
that there was no longer a solid core of men who were used
to building cars, knew what was involved in sweat and
labor, and wanted the jobs bad enough to turn up in fair
weather or foul, on time and ready to work a full day plus
as much overtime as would be needed to hit the production
quota. Absenteeism was fantastic — you were sure of having enough men to keep the line rolling only on payday —
and the turnover was something unbelievable unless you
stood there and watched the faces come and go, come and
go, in such numbers that you had to give up trying to learn

their names because most of them wouldn't stay long enough to make it worth while bothering.

"As soon as you try to get them to see just beyond their noses," he complained to his wife, "they take the attitude you're a company man. I pick up pieces of lead six and eight inches long that my solder flowers have thrown away because they can't be bothered flowing with a short stick, and I tell them the price of a hundred pounds of lead . . . and they laugh at me. I keep the sandpaper locked up according to instructions, and hand the boys out one piece at a time. They ask me why I'm so stingy, they ask me if I'm paying for it, and when I tell them that every single abrasive disc — the ones they toss around like kids with flying saucers — costs fifty cents, you know what they say?" He took a gulp of coffee. "They say, So what. You can't even get them to see that their jobs depend on keeping costs down. Even if you could, I don't think they'd care.

"Believe me, what the company did when they moved was to saddle us foremen with more headaches than we ever had. We're supposed to pull more production than at the old plant with a bunch of guys that walk in not knowing one end of a screwdriver from the other, and are just as apt to walk out at the end of the day and never show up again."

Agnes raised her eyes briefly from the stocking whose toe she was mending. She said mechanically, "It's a shame."

"It's asking too much. You can't make a quality product with just a mob. That's all you've got is a mob, different faces every day." Buster put down his coffee cup with a clatter and took off his glasses to wipe off the steam that had arisen from it. "Damn it, sometimes I wish they'd never built the new plant. We were all better off before."

Agnes smiled tolerantly. "Carl, you know that's silly. If it hadn't been for moving out to the country, we'd never have bought this nice house in a nice community, with Jeanie having a chance to meet refined boys and get away from the riffraff." She added hastily, "And with you not having to go far to work. It's worth putting up with some inconveniences when you think of the progress we've made just in this year alone. That's a sweet boy Jeanie's out with tonight, you know? A college boy."

"Inconveniences. What a word for the headaches I've got." Buster stood up and opened his belt. "Going to bed, Aggie. Sorry I can't wait up with you, but I'm beat."

For the first time, Agnes was stirred. She put down the stocking and raised her face for his kiss. "I feel bad for you, Carl. But it can't get worse, it has to get better. And if I was you I wouldn't let the company forget what I've been doing for them."

Buster smiled grimly to himself on the way to work the next morning as he recalled his wife's naïve bedtime comment. After all these years, she still didn't know the facts of life; it was lucky, he thought, that he'd taken her out of the beauty shop and insisted on her being a housewife.

When his men started coming in, he gave them each a hello as they ambled up from the time clock, opened their toolboxes and put on their aprons. It was always his policy to say hello and good-by to his men no matter how grumpy he or they felt. He wanted them to like him and respect him, not to fear or mistrust him. There were a few who understood, he was sure — men like Harold, the drunken artist, and old Pop, the inspector who had been around for a thousand years, and probably Orrin, his one good metal finisher, who was doubtless going to be made a boss one of these days; but they were a tiny minority. For the rest you had to keep the line going with men who — even if they grudgingly admired you — assumed that you were really there to make them sweat.

"Here," he would say to a new man standing around with his file dangling from his hand, trying to look interested, "let me show you how to use that. Guide it with your left hand. Keep your thumb and forefinger spread across the back of the file, and then just let it glide back and forth, like this. Don't rub, don't grip too hard. You know why?" he would smile at the awkward, nervous man. "Because this file can wear you down quicker than it can wear down the metal. Take it slow, easy and steady, remember to guide it, not force it, and you'll do fine."

The responses were varied, but Buster held to the patient approach, treating the newcomers, he explained, as he would have wanted to be treated himself. There were times when he lost his temper, mostly when the pressure was on and Hawks the body shop supervisor and some of the engineering wheels were standing around. Then he would yell and chew a man out for the work he'd left undone or the job he'd botched. Usually, however, he tried to stick to persuasion.

"Now look at that," he would say sadly, pointing to a low spot on a job one of his men had walked away from. "Would you buy that car?"

Or, when Hawks put the heat on him to have the men identify their work, he would pass among them with a box of chalk. "Don't make me tell you again," he would complain in as low a voice as possible. "They want to know which jobs are which. If you don't put your initials on every job you do, you'll wind up with a reprimand."

It seemed to him that the men on the line, even those who came and went like ghosts, must know that he was doing his best both to pull production and to cover for them, even when he screamed at them at the top of his lungs.

"Buster is the best boss in the shop." He had heard it with his own ears; he knew the word got around, and he knew that it was true.

He had constantly to be teaching these new men how to metal-finish, and as soon as one was well broken in, he would quit. That made no difference to the production men, who expected you to turn out forty units an hour if you had to do it singlehanded. And to top it off the job-study engineers began to make tests on his line. They tried having his metal finishers do every fourth job instead of every third, but do the entire side instead of only the rear quarter-

panel. This freed the metal finishers who had been special-
izing in front doors for other work, but it left Buster holding
a bagful of complaints from men who didn't like to work in
the first place and now felt that they had been tricked and
overburdened. All he could say was that experiments were
being made to expedite the work, and that nobody was
going to be asked to do more than he was capable of doing. But since most of the men were new and probationary
employees, they could not bitch to the union.

Buster did what he could. "I guess you don't believe it,"
he would say to a boy like Walter, who filed his heart out
but still did miserable work, "but I used to work myself.
Put in sixteen years before they made me a boss, so I know
how the workingman feels. Here, let me show you that, if
I can." And as Walter wiped his sweaty forehead on his
sleeve, Buster took up the file, buried his arm in the trunk,
and reached far forward to tap at the difficult dent, cheering the boy along as he showed him how to do it. "I
know exactly how it feels to have the damn things keep
coming one after the other. Sometimes you wish the line
would break down, right? What a wonderful feeling when
you look back and see a great big gap in the line between
the one you're finishing and the next one!" And he laughed
to see the boy flush guiltily.

But then the engineers decided to shake up yet another
operation. Two men put the cast-iron hooks and chains on
the cars on Buster's line: one hooked up the front ends,
the other the back, so that each car could be swung into

the air at the end of the line and floated into the bonderizing booth to be rust-proofed. These two men also fitted
on the lighter hooks on which the doors were hung for
both station wagons and panel trucks. Since their work
was heavy (the hooks and chains weighed about twenty
pounds apiece) but so unskilled that it could be learned in
two minutes by anyone with two hands and a strong back,
there was a tremendous turnover on the job. Already Buster had had a crazy Negro who sang at the top of his lungs,
an Irishman just in from the old country, several big, sad,
stupid men, and a number of crafty kids who didn't want
to do heavy work, or any work at all if they could help it.
The ones who quit, quit; from among the others Buster
picked out those who seemed to have some sense and set
them to work learning metal-finishing, which paid fifteen
cents an hour more than the crude work they were doing.
Always he knew, though, that the hook men were the easiest
to replace.

Now, however, the experts decided that the smaller hooks
could be installed at the very beginning of the line by the
man who gunned the door plates and had been clocked as
having time to spare. This left only the big chains and hooks
to be attached. It was the engineers' opinion that this
could be done by one man instead of two if he would pick
up one hook with each hand and mount the line between
two jobs, doing first the back of one car, then the front of
the car directly behind it on the line.

They explained it to Buster before the day's siren blew,

hitching up their belts beneath their white shirts and surrounding him aggressively, as if to shut off his complaints.

He said formally, "Those hooks get heavy."

"We've weighed them. They're well within the —"

"The point is that they get heavier as the day goes along. Especially if you ask a man to climb up and down with one in each hand. They're used to resting them against the stomach. You can't do that if you have to pick up two at a time."

"Let's try it," the little time-and-motion man said with finality. He raised his voice as the starting siren went off. "Where's your hook man?"

"I haven't got any yet. They took them both off to work in the duck pond yesterday. Horton is going to bring me a couple replacements from the employment office in a little while. Any minute."

They glanced at their stop watches. "We'll be back."

Then Horton, the production man, five years younger than Buster but five notches higher because he had an engineering degree and also, Buster was convinced, because he was a Mason like all the big wheels, came hustling up on his wiry bowlegs, towing along two new men, one old, one young. They stood at one side, new toolboxes in their hands, trying to look unconcerned as Horton spoke to Buster.

"Here's your men. You're only supposed to have one on the hooks."

"I know."

"Use the young kid for it. He's stronger."

Buster suppressed his anger. What kind of moron did Horton take him for?

"Besides," Horton finished, "the old boy's experienced. You won't hardly have to break him in." He lifted his hand abruptly in farewell and took off, humming as he bummed a ride on a passing engineer's bike.

Buster wheeled to examine the two men and discovered that the old boy, puffy and paunchy in his turned-up new dungarees, was staring at him with his head cocked to one side. He looked familiar.

"Say," Buster said tentatively, "don't I —"

"It's Frank, Buster. Frank's the name. I used to metal-finish when you were spot-welding, remember? It's been twenty years."

"Well, I'll be damned."

They shook hands. Clasping the older man's soft, tired hand, Buster found himself wondering why a man his age had to come back to work here after all these years. A little embarrassed, he said, "Welcome back."

"Thanks. I see a lot of faces —"

"Excuse me. The line's starting up, and I've got to get this other fellow going on the hooks. Start filing on the doors with that guy in the railroad cap, will you?" Buster turned to the glum youngster, who looked as though his mother had sent him off to work against his will. "Okay, put your gloves on, fellow, and I'll show you what I want of you."

He was a tall, doughy-faced Italian, with glittering black hair that he wore very long, completely covering the tops of his ears and meeting in back in what Buster had heard described as a duck's-ass haircut. His complexion was very white and bloodless, and the back of his neck above his shirt collar was pitted with deep, black-centered acne scars. Buster was a good Catholic and believed devoutly in not judging his fellow man by background or nationality, but he could not help thinking that this one looked like those neighborhood gang-warriors that you read about in the magazines; it wouldn't be surprising if he carried a six-inch switch-blade knife.

The boy observed Buster coldly, saying nothing, only muttering and nodding his head when Buster asked if he understood the work. After a few minutes the boy seemed to have caught on and Buster left him. He returned to Frank for a moment, faced with the problem of explaining that it would be impossible to stand around reminiscing about the old days. It was not easy to do this without playing the big shot or needlessly wounding an older man, and Buster found that he was starting to sweat. He told Frank to keep at it, to help him show the youngsters how you could work steady without killing yourself, and he moved on.

The next time he had a chance to look over the line and see how things were going — it must have been an hour later — he saw the Italian boy all the way up the line near the platform, twenty feet past where he should have been working. He was running sweat, and his oiled hair was falling over his ears. As Buster approached, he jerked his head angrily.

"How's it going?" Buster asked.

"I ain't Superman, Mac," the boy snarled, as he flung an iron chain into the rear of a station wagon with a crash.

"You can call me Buster. I'll help you get caught up." Buster half-trotted back to the head-high stack of hooks and chains that sat on a dolly at the middle of the line. Grabbing two, he hastened back to where he had been and hopped up onto the line. Crisscrossing each other, he and the boy had soon worked their way back to the center of the line.

"There you go," Buster said. He glanced down at the figured cotton sport shirt that Agnes had given him for his birthday — it was scored with red primer and dotted at the chest with droplets of sweat that had soaked through his undershirt. "Let's try to keep caught up, okay?"

"Christ," the boy said, and unloosed a torrent of obscene abuse on the factory and the entire auto industry. "I come in here to make a living, not to kill myself."

If the boy had looked and talked a bit differently, Buster would not only have sympathized with him, but would have tried to do something to lighten his load. As it was, he felt that the boy was swearing at him but didn't have the courage to do it directly. In the circumstances it was impossible to explain to the boy that he was being used as a guinea pig.

"Do the best you can," he said coldly. "You're entitled to twelve minutes' rest period before lunch. I'll check with the relief man to make sure you get your break."

"If I live that long," the boy replied.

Buster turned his back on him and sought out the relief man, who was doing Orrin's work.

"When Orrin comes back," he said, "get the new kid that's on the hooks. I don't want him griping that he didn't get his relief."

"When! When! How do I know when?" cried the relief man angrily. "Orrin cut his hand, he went to the hospital. He may be gone an hour. You want me to walk off his job here to make that kid happy?"

"Don't talk foolish. Stick with it, I'll see what I can do."

"You better not worry about the kid," the relief man warned as he bent to his work. "Better worry about all the guys that'll be on your neck for their relief if Orrin doesn't get back soon."

What the line needed, of course, was a utility man in addition to a relief man for just such situations, a good all-around man who could be slipped into any vacant slot in case of emergency. But the wheels wouldn't authorize the extra name on the payroll; they insisted that it was part of Buster's job to train up his men to cut down on accidents and minimize emergency situations.

Buster would just as soon have pitched in and given his men their relief himself, but it was against the union contract for a boss to touch a tool. He was uneasily aware that somebody with a grudge might be small enough to turn him in for working, even though he was getting a relief that he would not otherwise have had. Or maybe Lou the union committeeman would come by and cite him for the violation. Lou was looking for an excuse to demand the hiring of a utility man and make himself a big shot for the next election.

Buster decided to circulate among his men. "We're in a jam," he said. "Orrin's stuck in the hospital and I don't think you're going to get any relief this morning."

"No relief!" one shouted. "With them running forty-five jobs an hour at us! What the hell's going on here? If nobody's going to get his relief, shut the line down for twelve minutes and we'll all take it together."

"Let's be reasonable. You know I can't do anything like that. I'll see that you make it up. Maybe after lunch."

His men were not only working at a hard, steady pace themselves, but whenever they had a chance they lent a hand to the new man, handing him hooks and chains from the pile, sometimes doing a job themselves.

One of them complained bitterly, "That new kid can't keep up doing a two-man job, not with the line going this fast. Not even with our help."

It was true. The boy was sweating furiously, trotting, lifting, cursing steadily. One of the tails of his gaudy shirt had worked up in back and hung free over his trousers, which were, Buster now noticed, an old pair of dress pants cut in zoot style, billowing at the thigh and so tight at the cuff that his ankles seemed bound with bicycle clips. For some reason these draggy pants, which would have been at home in a candy store or a cheap saloon, not here where men were busy working hard, infuriated Buster. Still, he knew that he was being unfair, and he stepped back out into the aisle to see if he could spot the two engineers. Once they saw that they had miscalculated, he would be able to ask for another man.

But they were nowhere in sight. Naturally. He swore to himself and hurried back to the boy, who raised his head and yelled, "This isn't work, it's slavery!"

Two of the men on the line looked up and laughed. There was no question about whose side they were on, and it made Buster feel as though in some subtle, indefinable way they were betraying him by siding with such a punk.

Nevertheless, he grasped one of the elephant-tusk hooks and was preparing to help the boy to catch up once again when he heard his name being called. He looked up and saw Hawks standing fifty feet ahead, one hand hooked in the fancy woven belt which he claimed a lady friend had given him, the other hand waving imperiously for Buster to hurry. Above his brilliant tie of stars, planets, and asteroids whirling dizzily against the white universe of his shirt, his mournful, hangdog face was set for unpleasantness.

Another one of those Masons, Buster thought angrily as he stomped toward him. With no preamble the supervisor swung out his ringed hand and rapped it sharply against the taillight hole of a car swaying in the air between him and Buster.

"Let's tighten up a little, what do you say," he said. "See if you can get your boys to understand that we've got to meet competition. Jobs like this one here can't go through."

It was true. There was an unchalked dent down low, below the taillight; but since it had slipped by Pop the inspector it was understandable that it should have been missed. Buster looked at the front of the job: it bore Orrin's initials. He put two fingers to his mouth and whistled up the relief man who was doing Orrin's work.

With deliberate slowness the relief man straightened up from his job and slouched forward to meet him. "Listen, Buster," he said flatly, ignoring the supervisor, who did not move but simply turned his back on them, "they're coming fast, and I got a lot of work. Can't your pick-up men take care of the little things we miss?"

"This isn't little." Buster pointed to the dent with his cigar. "You ought to know better than to let a job like this go by. You're getting a dime an hour extra for being a relief man. You want to keep on getting that dime, you better do the work right. Come on, clean it up and get back to your place."

The relief man flashed him a look of pure hatred. But he said nothing, instead dropped to one knee, inserted his arm with the file inside the taillight hole, and began to rap rhythmically at the dent. Buster stood watching him for a moment. He could think of nothing to say that would take the sting out of what he had just said, and so at last he turned to Hawks.

"I'm shorthanded today," he said to the supervisor, "and they're trying to make the hooks a one-man job, and —"

"Shorthanded? Didn't they give you two new men? I saw the schedule sheet myself."

"Yes, but one is going to metal-finish. He's too old for the hooks anyway, and the other one is breaking his hump. He just can't keep up."

"I know you like to stick up for your men." Hawks pulled a pendulous earlobe and stared at him sadly. "That's fine. Now try sticking up for me a little. I've got to turn out three hundred and fifty units before the night shift comes on. Think about that. Next time you see Horton, give him your complaint."

Thus dismissed, Buster returned to the line, grabbed a hook, and hopped up to give the new boy a hand.

The boy was a mess. He had not put on an apron, and his front was splotched with red primer dust. His face was blotched with red, and with hatred and self-pity, and he muttered to himself unceasingly as he strove. My God, Buster thought, a crazy colored singer, a crazy Irish schoolteacher, a dozen assorted morons, and now a teen-age bum.

"Tell you something," he said to the boy as they stood back to back on the moving line, working together. "I know what it is to work. Don't think I don't sympathize with you.

I used to work. I worked for sixteen years before they made me a boss. And I had plenty of rough days like you're having now. It's all part of the game."

"Sixteen *years*," the boy sneered incredulously. "You must have been some quick thinker."

Buster clamped his jaws shut tight. He jumped off the line and lifted up another hook. Panting a little now, he said, "Jobs weren't as easy to come by in those days as they are now. If you made a living you were grateful, and you hung on."

"Times have changed."

"They sure have," Buster said. "But I haven't. I started working when I was fourteen, and I worked too long and too hard to forget what it's like. That's why I feel I'm still just one of the boys in spite of the fact that I've been a boss for nine years."

"Who did you get to know after those sixteen years?" the boy asked insolently. "Or did you just wait for somebody to die off?"

Buster bit hard on his cigar. "You want to get anyplace in this world," he said coldly, "you better learn to smarten up."

The boy laughed as he flung back his long black hair. "I was *born* smarter," he replied, "than some of the characters around this dump."

Shortly after that, the man gunning the door plates ran out of screws; then an air hose broke and whirled lethally through the air, hissing and twirling madly like a crazed snake; one thing followed another, and Buster had no more chance to help the new boy. Once he glanced up and saw that although the boy was again so far behind that he was running from one end of the fast-moving line to the other, staggering under the weight of the hooks he carried, the other men, furious at being cheated out of their relief and at the way the boy was being treated, were giving him a hand whenever they could spare a few seconds. Finally Orrin came back from the hospital, and the relief man was freed to give some rest to at least a few of the men.

When the siren blew for lunch, Buster had no appetite. He bought a bowl of stew and a cup of coffee and sat down at his customary place with the foreman from the grinding booth and Halstein, boss inspector.

The grinding booth foreman looked at him sympathetically. "Tough day today, Buster?" he demanded between gulps of soup.

Buster opened his mouth to tell them and then thought better of it. He crumbled a cracker into the stew and shrugged. "The usual."

Then Halstein, who Buster suspected stood in well with the Masonic clique, started to talk about a three-dimensional kite his boy had built, and Buster hardly listened. His eyes were searching for the little time-study man, who slipped in and out of the cafeteria like a ghost. At last Buster spotted him, two minutes before they had to return. He hastened over to him.

"You fellows changed that operation into a one-man deal

on my line," he said quickly, "but you never came around to check on it."

"Tied up," the little engineer said tersely.

"Now look, it's just too much for one man. I'm short-handed as it is. I told you before —"

"We'll get to you this afternoon. Keep your shirt on."

How could Agnes or anyone on the outside know how it was to be caught in the middle between zoot-suiters and college hot shots? Sometimes, he thought, the advantages didn't outweigh the headaches, not at all; and he could understand the men who had turned down chances to be made foremen, or who had given up foremen's jobs and returned to production, where they were covered by the union and had no such worries, or had transferred into plant protection, where all they had to do was wear uniforms and look important. At his desk he lit a fresh cigar and, as the line started to roll once again, busied himself with the attendance sheets that had to be cleaned up. He had been at it for perhaps ten minutes and was just about finished when something, some instinctive feeling that all was not right, made him swivel about and stare.

For a moment everything looked normal. The line was going at a fairly fast clip and his men, their stomachs full, were working hard and steady. Then he realized what was wrong. None of the cars, not one of them, had any hooks on it — and the new boy was nowhere in sight.

His heart hammering, Buster leaped forward and took the nearest man by the arm.

"Where's that hook man? The new one?"

The metal finisher had an odd glint in his eye. "I haven't seen him since lunch."

"Why didn't you tell me?" Then seeing the man's face stiffen, "Never mind. Run down there and tell the relief man to come up here."

Without waiting, Buster grabbed two hooks and hurled them onto the station wagons before which he had been standing. If he did not get caught up within a very few minutes, the cars reaching the head of the line without hooks would not be able to swing off; they would pile up, and the entire line would have to be stopped. And it was on his neck.

Blindly, cursing the missing boy, Buster flung himself at the hooks and fastened them to the cars, bending over double in his haste. The blood rushed to his head and the vein in his left temple began to pound. He finished two jobs and ran headlong back to the stack of hooks for two more, his key ring falling from his pocket as he ran.

"What's on your mind, Buster?" the relief man asked him coolly.

Without pausing, Buster said over his shoulder, "Take over for me, will you, until I can find that son of a —"

"I'm not going to hang hooks all afternoon. I'm not paid for that. I'm not even supposed to relieve the hook man and you know it."

"It's not for all day. Just till that guy turns up."

"I doubt that he will. Somebody heard him say he was pulling out."

"*What!*"

"Sorry, Buster." The relief man's small eyes glittered maliciously. "Most of your men got no relief this morning. I can't gyp them out of it this afternoon too just because this kid took off." He sauntered away.

Buster did not dare to stop to hunt for help. As he passed another of his men kneeling with his file, he cried out, "Where's the new guy?"

And this man, too, grinned. "I hear he didn't even punch out. Just hit the road."

Trying to keep from growing panicky, Buster clambered stiffly onto the line with the two hooks and tried to consider how he could get word to supervision that he needed help quickly. A glance up and down showed no one in sight. His own men looked as though they could hardly keep their faces straight.

"I wouldn't mind," he said to the man kneeling below him, "if he'd only told me." He tried to keep his voice casual. "It's a free country. Nobody can make you work if you don't want to. But to sneak out without letting anybody know . . ."

"It just shows you," the crouching man yelled up at him. "Even a crummy job like that, a job nobody wants and any dope can do, you got to treat a man right to do it right or you can't build cars."

"You're not telling me anything I don't know," Buster

cried angrily, as he straightened his back and scrambled off the line. "All I ask is my men play square with me like I try to play square with —"

At that instant a booming crash rang out over all the other noises of the body shop. Everyone looked up at once, bewildered. The crash was followed by a horrible sound of rending metal. Then Buster knew what had happened. He was petrified inside with the positive knowledge that more was to follow; his tongue was frozen into silence; but his body continued to move automatically. Yes, it came again, another crash like the first, followed by more rhythmic thuds, until everyone on the line realized what was happening.

The Italian boy had taken his vengeance before running away. He had attached the hooks and chains of his last few jobs lopsidedly, in some cases only fastening one side, so that now, an hour after he had escaped, the cars tilted as they entered the narrow bonderizing booth, and, hanging off balance, crashed back and forth, back and forth, against the sides of the booth, metal smashing against metal as the cars were systematically pounded out of shape.

When the third car had begun to rocket back and forth in the booth, Buster, the sweat streaming down his cheeks, saw Hawks and Horton and two other white-shirted executives from quality control running down the aisle and clambering up the catwalk to the little metal door in the center of the bonderizing booth. Then a battery-powered scooter rolled up and the assistant plant superintendent hopped off, followed by three overalled maintenance men.

Now that it was too late, the reinforcements had arrived.

Up and down the line his men, looking like strangers, were openly grinning. With every booming thud, every tearing sound, their grins grew wider. They didn't care that hundreds of dollars in time and labor were going down the drain; it amused them. They didn't care that the smashed hulks would have to be hauled out of the booth and dragged to a corner; they were already calculating the overtime they would earn repairing these wrecks. They didn't care that he was still hanging hooks, with the weight of them starting to stab in his groin, unable to summon help from the bosses, who now had something more important to keep them occupied. They thought he had it coming, and Buster, his heart wrenched in his chest, stared at their grinning faces and wondered how it could be that people who worked together could have so little human feeling. Don't they know I couldn't help it? he asked himself.

"Hey, Buster!" one of them called out. "Some symphony, eh?"

"Laugh," he replied grimly. "We may all get laid off for this."

"Say, Buster — how does it feel to work like a dog? Does it take you back to the old days? The good old days?"

Tossing a heavy hook contemptuously into the rear of a station wagon, he faced them out and said coolly, around his cigar, "I've worked harder, in my time. I never asked one man, never in my life, to do a job I wouldn't do."

The cigar tasted rancid in his gummy mouth, but it was a visible proof that he had not capitulated, that he was simply handling a passing crisis; so he refused to throw it away, or even to take it out of his mouth while he worked. But he could not prevent the sweat from pouring down his body, from forming huge, dark, telltale moons under the armpits of his sport shirt, from plastering the front of the shirt to his chest, from soaking through his slacks at the base of his spine, from dripping down his forehead onto the rims of his glasses, smudging and steaming the lenses.

He hated to do it, but, half-blinded by his own sweat, he had to take off the glasses and stuff them into his shirt pocket. In a way it was worse than giving up the cigar would have been. Without the glasses he felt naked and exposed, and he knew that his face took on a stupid, blinking expression when his nearsighted eyes tried to adjust themselves to an uncorrected world.

On one of the passing panel trucks someone had scrawled in huge letters, no doubt with the chalk that he himself had handed out, TOO MANY CHIEFS, NOT ENOUGH INDIANS!

"I bet you'll sleep good tonight, eh, Buster?" somebody asked as he hurried off the line to lift up a hook.

"A little hard work never killed anybody," he muttered around his dead cigar. But his groin was tight as a drumhead, and every step counted off every month of his forty-five years.

"Wait'll we get the union after you, Buster!" someone called out.

He whirled about but could not see who had said it; they all had their heads down. There wasn't one of them would complain to their committeeman, not because they feared reprisals, but because this show was too good to put an end to.

Oh, they'd have something to talk about all the way home, and even after they got home — how the boss had been humiliated and made to work like a dog.

I'm through, he said to himself; I'll turn in my time and ask for a transfer; I can make my living without having to take this. Glancing down at the red primer dust which covered him, he could already hear his wife's voice added to all the rest.

"Kind of rough, hey, Buster?" It was Orrin, the only man on the line with a perfect attendance record; the only one who really liked hard work and hard pressure. "They won't hold you responsible. It wasn't your fault that young jerk ducked out."

Buster mumbled a reply. He was unsure whether these first words of sympathy he'd had all day were sincere or whether Orrin, having gotten wind of his possible promotion, was starting to suck around.

Old Frank, who had been doing a great job of making himself inconspicuous, now sidled up to him, encouraged maybe by what Orrin had just said. He cleared his throat and spat into the lead filings.

"Say listen, Buster," he said gruffly, "can I spell you on that job? I'm not doing too much metal-finishing."

"That's all right, Frank. Just stick at what you're doing, I want you to get the feel of it again."

"But I'll tell you frankly, I didn't think I'd get back in here at my age, and I'd like to show my appreciation, so if you'd let me —"

"No, no, that's all right, thanks. You get days like this, and you just have to learn to live with them."

Fortunately at that moment Horton and the quality-control man came over from the bonderizing booth, and Frank had to do a fade-out. They seemed to think the scene was pretty funny, too, and they stood there, grinning, watching him sweat.

"You certainly must have browbeat that kid to make him walk out after four hours," Horton said. "Man, what a slave driver."

"I understand Accounting is going to bill you for the prorated extra labor cost on those four banged-up jobs," the quality-control man said.

"Very funny," Buster snarled. "Are you going to get me a man for this job or not?"

The quality-control man turned to Horton. "Didn't you hear them say Buster was going to have to work it off until he'd made up for his sins?"

"All right, all right," Horton said, smiling at his Masonic buddy, then turning to Buster. "Come on down off that line, they're getting you a replacement. You look like hell if I may say so, like Before in the Before and After ads."

It was true. Buster stared at himself in the washroom

mirror when he had gone in to clean up for a minute, after they'd provided him with another man to finish out the day. He looked like Before, but he felt like After, long After. And what would you do if you threw it over? Who could you tell to go to hell? Yourself? That nameless herd who came and went like stockyard cattle? That clique of Masons who boosted each other and each other's relatives into all the key jobs, and would maybe one day make him an assistant supervisor, or a foreman over the body shop foremen, just to satisfy the Michigan crowd that they were bringing up men from the ranks?

When the day was over at last, he sat down for a while in the body shop office and went over with Hawks and several others the series of events that had been so costly to him and to production, but wouldn't even rate a footnote in the history of the corporation. They gave him to understand that it was a closed issue, dead and forgotten, if he would see to it in the future that such things wouldn't happen again.

Weary and pensive, he got in his car and crawled home to the new development where his house stood on an artificially winding black-top road, in the middle of what had been a potato field two years before. As he coasted up the driveway he caught sight of his wife outside the kitchen door, hanging the laundry on the aluminum and nylon-cord dryer that he'd mounted in concrete for her, a temporary expedient which would have to be replaced one day soon by an automatic dryer.

She looked pretty, her arms raised against the twilight, her shy lips puckered with clothespins, her skirt whipping free — younger and slimmer than she really was. She waved at him, and he waved back, but he was too tired to talk or to kiss her, and he went directly into the house and drew himself a tub.

Flat on his back with the water still bubbling at his ankles, he found himself thinking of old Frank. That was probably the most important thing that had happened during the day — Frank's showing up after twenty years, ready and willing to take up a job that wasn't good enough for that teen-age gangster. But when Agnes asked him — as she would — what had happened at the shop, he wasn't going to be able to tell her about Frank. She would say that it was a shame, a man of fifty-six having to start in all over, and of course that was true; she would wonder what had happened after all these years to make him come back to the shop, and that was something to wonder about, it was true; but she would also end by gloating a little and by pointing out the contrast and the fact that Buster might still move up yet another notch or two if his luck held. And that he wasn't ready to say at all.

Because no one could know; there were things you couldn't say and things you shouldn't say; and maybe at that moment when Frank had offered to help out he was in a stronger position than Buster himself . . . even though it was also true that the very sight of him with his old belly and his new work pants was enough to drive out of Buster's mind any serious thought of giving up his foreman's job.

He sighed, and heard his wife's voice outside the door, above the running water: "Everything all right, Carl?"

"Yes."

"Have a hard day?"

"I had a lousy day."

"What? What did you say?"

He turned up the water and splashed a bit so as not to have to answer, and his wife went on. "We've got to talk about that summer bungalow before Jeanie gets home, because I've got to mail in the deposit tonight. I've been thinking — can you hear me, Carl? — it might be worth while to invest in one in a better location where there's a better class of boys. I know you've got your heart set on that boat, but maybe if we took the *boat* money and put it toward the *bungalow,* it would pay off as far as Jeanie's concerned, and maybe next summer if you get a promotion we can think about that boat again . . ."

He closed his eyes, took his nose by thumb and forefinger, and eased himself under the circling water. When he came up his wife had stopped talking, and he stepped from the tub, cleaner at least, to prepare himself for dinner and the evening.

EIGHT

Back in the Saddle Again

A S RECENTLY as a decade ago,' it says, 'a man of sixty-five was considered old. Now, as increasing medical knowledge and an ever-higher standard of living push back the frontiers of age, we —' "

"Oh please, May." Her husband raised his hands wearily from the solitaire game spread out before him. "I know all that by heart."

"I didn't mean to break up your train of thought."

"It's not that." He looked at his wife, short, squat, warm-bosomed, smiling anxiously behind the gleaming bifocals, her two-strap shoes planted firmly on the carpet; she seemed to be growing out of the couch like a mushroom. He sighed. I'm fat myself, he thought; but after thirty-three years May still thinks of us as honeymooners. "If men of seventy aren't old any more, then what's somebody like me? A kid of fifty-six. That's what you're getting at, isn't it?"

"Don't poke fun at me, Frank. I just can't stand to see you down in the dumps."

Frank found himself longing to turn on the television. There was nothing he wanted to see; there was nothing he had against his wife's talking. It was simply that, sitting here in their son's parlor and minding the grandchildren, they had come to the end of the road. The business was shot, the bills were overdue, and the account was overdrawn. They both knew and dreaded what came next, but while May was still game for dream-answers, Frank wanted only to drown himself in the television.

"Don't you want to talk, Frank? Because if you don't, I won't disturb you any more."

May was fairly shrewd. The boys were sleeping soundly, and she knew that this was the best time to talk, before Ray and his wife came home. Besides, Ray would probably have his cousin Wilbur with him — everything hinged on Wilbur. Frank scooped up the cards, smoothed them out, and slipped them into their case.

"All right," he said to his wife, folding his hands on the card table and looking at her steadily. "What it comes down to is that you think I've quit and that I think it's time to face reality. I'm just not young enough to gamble other people's money on new business deals. You can't talk me into feeling different just because you don't want me to go back to the factory."

"But that's what I don't understand. If you're too worn out for business, how are you going to be able to take the assembly line?"

"Here's where I'm tired." He touched his temple with his fingertip. "I can't take any more lickings in business, May. The only security for us is for me to go back to the factory, union or no union, labor or no labor. Isn't that clear by now?"

"But the drive-ins," she said desperately. "You said yourself they're the coming thing in the picture business."

"They're out of my class. I can handle popcorn stands in neighborhood movies, but drive-ins? It takes dough to make dough, and I haven't got the nerve to borrow any more. Besides . . ." He hesitated. "Who'd lend me the money?"

The silence was painful. May knew the answer as well as he. Her family had loaned Frank the equity price of the appliance franchise twenty years ago, and on the strength of it he had quit the factory. He had learned how to reduce an inventory but not how to handle money, so he was caught and slowly drained out in the credit squeeze. It had taken him a long time and some painful side lines (door-to-door selling of tableware was one), to pay off that debt. Later he had borrowed again, first from his own family, then from the bank as he prospered, to go into the candy concession business. Right through the war he did fine. But when it ended, instead of pulling in his horns he had expanded, buying into an entire chain just in time for the collapse of the movie industry. He had become a little tycoon in town, a real chain operator, and before his eyes the chain rusted away, eating up with it his capital and most of his life savings. Even if money weren't tight now, the banks wouldn't give him a break, not after his big miscalculation. There was only one source left.

A bolder man might have done it, might have gone to his children and his nephews, to the young ones who were on the way up and had a little put aside, and asked them for a stake. The killing was there to be made, May was right, if you were bold; but he was no longer willing to take the risk.

May said anxiously, "You still didn't answer me, how you're going to be able to work on the assembly line again after twenty years. It's not like standing behind a candy counter. I'll never forget what you went through, those eleven years in the factory. You got old before your time. How long do you think you'll last this time?"

"Conditions are different now," he replied with false heartiness. "They got civilized, these last twenty years. If you don't believe me, ask Wilbur. He's in Personnel, it's true, but he's in and out of the shop ten times a day. Besides . . . what alternative have I got?"

The look in May's eyes was terrible, so terrible that neither of them could bear it, and after an instant they both lowered their eyes in confusion, like two strangers who bump on a sidewalk and then veer away from one another. Then, thank God, one of the boys started to cry.

"It's Jerry," May murmured.

"Let me take care of him," Frank said eagerly.

"Bring him a glass of water. Maybe he only wants to be covered, but take the water just in case."

Puffing a little, Frank approached the crib of his four-year-old grandson. The little boy had quieted at his approach and sat waiting in the dark.

"Want a drink of water, Jerry?"

Jerry did not speak, but instead nodded with such vigor that his blond curls fell forward across his forehead. Aching with love, Frank bent down and handed him the glass, holding on so that it would not spill. His fingers met his grandson's and enfolded them until the glass was empty.

"Now cover me good." Even as he spoke, the boy fell back asleep.

Frank was tiptoeing out of the room when Jerry's older brother startled him by speaking in a conversational voice.

"Say, Grandpa, would you tuck me in too?"

"Shh," he replied automatically as he approached the bed of his eight-year-old grandson. "You don't want Jerry to wake up again, do you?"

Donnie's black eyes glittered happily, catching the reflection of the dim hall light. "Don't worry about *him*. He even drinks that water in his sleep. But he's cute, isn't he?"

Frank's heart turned over. He dropped to one knee to arrange the dark-haired boy's covers. "Going to give me a kiss?"

Donnie flung his arms around his neck and whispered, "What are you and Grandma doing inside?"

"Just talking."

"I know, I heard you. But what about?"

Frank sought words. "About what I'm going to do. I may take a position in the automobile plant where your Uncle Wilbur works. I used to work there many, many years ago, before you were born."

"Are you going to do what Uncle Wilbur does?"

"No . . . It'll be something a little different."

"Can I come and visit you?"

"We'll see," he responded automatically. He smoothed the boy's fine dark hair back from his forehead. "Now go to sleep."

May glanced up from her paper as he entered the living room. "Everything all right?"

"Sure." He sat down next to her on the sofa. It was one of those modern ones, so close to the ground that his knees seemed to come up toward his jaw. "May, don't be upset. You know I'm just trying to be practical. It isn't even sure that Wilbur can get me in, they seldom take men over thirty-five these days."

"Well, I hope they don't." Her face was set. "You think it means nothing to me, what you went through with all those low-class people when they were organizing the union — those beatings, fights, cars being tipped over. I'll never forget how you hated it. How can you go back?"

"They don't remember me any more. All that business

is settled now." How he wished he could believe what he was saying! "Let me worry about that. The point is, you can't laugh off the security. I've got ten years left to build up my Social Security. Now Wilbur thinks those eleven years I put in will count towards my retirement rights. You realize what that means? In ten years I'll be able to quit for good. We wouldn't have much, but we could get by without being dependent. As it is now . . ."

May folded the paper and put it between them. "I want you to promise me one thing," she said. "Just one thing."

He rubbed his bald head and squinted at her warily. "What?"

"Promise me that if it gets too hard you'll quit. It isn't worth it — to wear yourself out and get mixed up in union fights for a pittance, a little pension. Do you promise?"

He nodded silently.

May reached for his hand. Glancing down in surprise, he saw her pudgy little fingers with the two rings disappearing into his own.

"Those little kids are beautiful, you know?" he asked after a while.

"Look who they take after!" May laughed.

They were sitting companionably over May's crossword puzzle when Ray and his cousin Wilbur came in with their wives.

"Well! Good evening, Lovebirds," Ray said amiably, as he helped the women off with their coats. "The kids give you any trouble, Dad?"

"They never stirred." Frank arose and knocked out his pipe. "Wilbur, May and I have been talking it over, and we've decided to go ahead with the factory idea — if you still think you can swing it."

The younger people were elaborately casual. Frank knew at once that they too had just been speaking of his situation. It hurt. Which was worse — to be the boy who was in a cold sweat over his father or the father who knew what he was doing to his boy? Ray had nothing to offer his father but sympathy — and even that, Frank knew, he dared not express but had instead to pretend that it meant nothing to him — or even that he was pleased — that his father was going to wind up as he had started, an overalled factory worker.

As for Wilbur, Frank's late brother's only child, he had two alternatives, neither of them pleasant. He could gamble one last time on his uncle by loaning him all the money he had, or he could plead with the plant to make an exception and take on a man of fifty-six because he was a deserving relative. As soon as he began to speak, smiling softly and smoothing down his rain-soaked moustaches, Frank knew which of the unpleasant courses Wilbur preferred.

"Of course I can, Uncle. Why don't you come in about ten tomorrow? That'll give me an hour or two to prep the boys and sort of grease the way for you." He was very decent about it; he made it seem as if it was nothing at all, when in fact Frank realized perfectly well that it was going to be an extremely embarrassing thing for him to pull off, bucking the actuarial tables and probably begging his boss to break a regulation.

So Frank said, "I'm very grateful to you, Wilbur," and then he and May got into their coats and went out into the rain.

Wilbur had greased the way so well that Frank, sucking in his guts tensely and trying to look eager, but not too eager, was through the mill and back on the payroll almost before he could believe it.

May was ashamed, but she was brave enough to face out their friends; she was anxious, those first few days, to know exactly how it was with him. When he lay back in his lounge chair, his slippered feet burning and his back sorer than he could admit, Frank tried to put it in words.

"You walk in and pick up your tools and it's exactly the same as it was twenty years ago. Same smells, same noises, same assembly lines. I'm back in the body shop, just like I was, as if I'd only been gone a week end instead of twenty years. Yet . . . it's all different, and not just because they've put up this new plant, or got a lot of automatic equipment."

"I hope you don't work as hard as you used to."

"Nobody does. I don't know if it's my imagination, but everybody seems younger. They haven't got any idea what it was like in the old days. Oh, you work, you still work like a dog, but that fear of being thrown out in the street isn't there. Once you've got your ninety days in, the union protects you." He looked sidewise at his wife. "Maybe I should have made more allowances, back in the thirties, for what they were up against, trying to civilize the company."

"They weren't very civilized themselves."

"They wouldn't let you be neutral, that's what it came down to. And when you see how different it is now . . . I feel a little funny, coming back after all this time to ride the gravy train."

Actually he felt even funnier than he said. He felt funny about being a recipient of the benefits the union had won; and he felt the weight of the twenty years in which he had been a man of business, wearing a white shirt every day and working with his wits instead of his back. It seemed to him that everyone must be looking askance at him: the union men gloating over the downfall of someone who had been too good for them and who now crawled back to be a free-loader in his old age; his friends and neighbors shaking their heads smugly over his degradation; and his own family, even his little grandchildren, humiliated by his final entrapment in the dirty pit from which he had made his escape earlier, only to fall back into it again now, once and for all.

During these first days, while he was being shifted from job to job, he hunted instinctively for men who had sweated and suffered with him in the old days and would perhaps appreciate how he felt about re-entering their world and how he reacted to both permanence and change.

He found them, but they too had changed. Buster, the

boss to whom he had been assigned, had worked on the line with him twenty years before as a spot welder — but Buster was a boss like all factory bosses, living in the present with a vengeance, worried, harried, frightened. None of the bosses who had worked with Frank as youngsters could relax and reminisce about the days when they were all young and beating their brains out on the line. He became convinced that they simply would not fraternize, partly to make it clear to him that he wasn't on an equal footing with them now, and partly because they felt sorry for him; curious — but afraid to ask — why he had been forced to come back to this work at his age.

There were a few who hadn't moved up at least a notch. Like Old Pop, however, they had soured from standing around too long. Utterly incurious, they didn't give a damn about what you'd been doing all these years; they had nothing to tell you about what they'd been doing. It was written all over their faces anyway: they were waiting for retirement. But my God, Frank groaned to himself, why else am *I* here?

So he avoided the men of his generation at least as much as they avoided him. Instead he mixed with boys thirty years and more younger than he. They listened, they asked questions, and, even if they were utterly lacking in respect for his years, they made him feel that he was part of what was going on around him. In turn they wanted gossip about what their bosses had been like in the old days.

"By and large," Frank would say to the youngsters,

"every boss you see around here, with the exception of Buster, was a company man back in the days when I worked with them."

"How about Blatnik, the boss over in the grinding booth?"

"What about Halstein, the boss inspector?"

"Two of the worst." Frank turned down the corners of his mouth and nodded heavily. "They'd turn in their own buddies just to get in good with the bosses. And you can't imagine what the bosses were like. One of them caught a man smoking in the john. The man quick tossed his butt in the toilet and flushed it, but the boss reached in with his whole arm, soaking and all, and pulled the butt out for evidence. Got the man fired too, a poor Indian by the name of Snowflake."

"You're kidding."

Frank drew himself up. "No story I could invent would do this place justice. You fellows don't know what dog-eat-dog means. Ask Buster about Snowflake, some time when he's not busy, and see what he says."

But then Buster did come along and broke them up. The line started to move again, and one smooth-cheeked solder flower, flipping his goggles down over his eyes and flaring the flame of his gun, said fiercely, "You can't tell me you worked any harder in those days than we do now."

Frank looked at him incredulously. "We were getting sixty-two and a half cents an hour and damn glad to get it, it was big money. You know what we did for that money? You got any idea how fast this line moved? It was nothing to see them sending the jobs down one a minute, and so close to each other you couldn't possibly get in between them to do your work. But it wasn't just that, it was the fear."

"Fear of what?"

"They called the foremen pushers in those days." Frank ran his file slowly back and forth over a high spot on the station wagon before him. He said ruminatively, "You should have heard the way they talked."

"You think they're any different now?" The solder flower flicked off his gun, pushed his goggles up onto his forehead, and fixed Frank with his young, intent blue eyes. "A guy the other day told me something that made me laugh. Hawks, the body shop supervisor, happened to notice. He went over to Buster and said, 'We're not paying that man for standing around and grinning. Tell him to get to work, he's supposed to be flowing solder, not smiling.' I went over to him and said, 'If you've got something to tell me, tell it to me yourself.' He just looked at me, disgusted, and walked away. But the very next day the assistant superintendent of the whole damn day shift came over in his little buggy and sat in it, right there in the aisle, watching me work for a solid hour without taking his eyes off me. Once I said something to the guy next to me, and he called me over and said, 'We're not paying you for conversation. Do your work on the job and your talking on your lunch hour.' It's lucky he drove off, I would have slugged him."

"Now let me tell *you* something. In the old days if you'd opened a mouth like that, you'd have been out in the street like a shot. Those pushers would walk right alongside of you as you worked, laughing at the way you were sweating and not even giving you time to wipe it off. 'What's the matter?' they'd yell. 'Can't you keep up? There's five thousand men waiting outside the gates for your job, so if you don't want the money, just say so.' They'd keep it up on you all day long, riding you, screaming at you, 'Five thousand men waiting, five thousand men waiting!' And there were, too. Believe me, there were."

That silenced the boy. I'm talking like a union agitator, Frank thought, but what's true is true. The years in business, bad ones and good ones, when he had been a man among men, scheming, figuring, dreaming, guessing, gambling, succeeding and failing, had absorbed him to the point where he had completely buried the eleven murderous years on the assembly line; but now that he was here once again, the flood of reminiscence was so turbulent that he could not keep it confined.

Sitting in the great humming cafeteria with five hundred strangers around him, all talking, eating, smoking, and shouting at once, he raised his eyes from his lonely plate to observe a plant policeman, resplendent in powder-blue uniform, stroll in from the bosses' cafeteria and pose motionless in the doorway.

Instantly every sound ceased and there was a moment of complete silence, as when the curtain lifts and a solitary figure is seen on stage, ready to begin the play. Then instead of a storm of applause came a hurricane of catcalls, of boos and stamping feet. The guard, a chunky, red-faced little man, thrust his thumbs deeper into his Sam Browne belt and stood his ground, his face turning redder, creased by a half-apologetic, half-proud smile.

"This happen often?" Frank asked the man on his right.

"Every time he sticks his nose in here. Kind of like those prison scenes in the movies, isn't it?"

Frank nodded absently. "Those guards used to be the worst elements, the dregs. I've seen them pick up a man bodily and carry him past the gates, crying and kicking. They had no respect for any human being, they were like a bunch of trained dogs." But when Frank paused, he realized that the man to whom he had been speaking was no longer listening.

At home May listened, but he did not want to tell her how the job brought back all the garbage of the past. "The main thing," he said to her, "is for me to get over that ninety-day hump. As it is, I'm still probationary and I never know from one day to the next what I'll be doing."

In plain truth, Frank was frightened. Wilbur was being transferred to the West Coast. If Management felt like taking back the favor they had done, there would be nothing and no one to stop them. And if I'm not good enough for this, what will I do then? Frank asked himself in the dead of the night, fagged and aching beside his softly snoring wife. If they dump me, what then?

"Grandpa," Donnie asked, "what do you *do* in the auto factory?"

"It's . . . hard to explain, without getting technical. What I do — well, it has to do with preparing the automobiles to be painted." Frank added, with hearty vagueness, "It's mighty complicated, putting together all those cars."

"Well, I'll find out soon. Our class is going on a tour through the factory some day next week." The pointed, questing face turned up trustingly. "And I'm going to look for you, Grandpa, and then I'll be able to prove to my friends that you make all those new cars, like I told them in Show and Tell!"

From then on his working day became not just physically wearing, but nervously exhausting too. With Wilbur gone, Frank had no assurance that he would be kept on. Now he also had to keep an eye out for each party of tourists that passed through the body shop, fearful that Donnie and his classmates would come upon him unawares.

Watching for Donnie, he was made painfully aware of the contrast between himself and the businessmen who came down the aisles, staring curiously about them and nudging one another as they strolled. Escorted by a joking company guide, they stepped carefully so as not to soil their trousers, laughing among themselves, adjusting the name cards that adorned their lapels and gazing not so much at the working men as at the autos in various stages of completion.

Frank grew panicky every time he saw tourists approaching. He shrank down, he opened the door of the car on which he was working and cowered behind it, he blew his nose with a large handkerchief; what if a group of conventioning candy jobbers were to come through and spot him? Even if they said nothing, even if they controlled their faces and smiled politely, the thought of how they would speak of him after they had passed out of earshot was enough to make Frank cringe inside his work clothes.

One morning he was stuck on a job just at the aisle as a guided group came along. There was nothing for it; he had to go on with what he was doing under the eyes of salesmen who wore starched French cuffs and smelled of shaving lotion. Down on one knee like a supplicant, he filed away dazedly and heard with humming ears the comments of the laughing visitors as they moved their polished shoes only a few feet beyond his hands. As he looked up from the stained concrete against which his knee throbbed, one of them broke free from the group and advanced to the line.

"Tell me honestly now," he demanded of the metal finisher working beside Frank, "which make of car would you recommend my buying?"

"You know something? That *is* an embarrassing question!"

The salesman broke out in a guffaw. "D'you hear that?" he cried out after his group, trotting to catch up as they passed the bonderizing booth. "D'you hear what he said?"

"For God's sake," Frank said to the boy, "what'd you want to say a thing like that for?"

The metal finisher looked at him, puzzled. "What the hell's the difference? It was just a joke."

He was right. But why do *I* care? Frank asked himself.

There were two reasons. He was still living in the old days, when you could have gotten fired on the spot for talking like that; but more important, and worse, he was ashamed of what he did. His new work clothes were already stained, spotted, and torn; his undershirt, showing out above the neck of his blue cotton shirt, was brown-rimmed, not because he wore it too long but because his perspiration, chemically affected by the lead in the air, stained underclothing, sheets, and pillow cases, even after he had bathed. With his scant hair disheveled and gritty, he looked like nothing more than what he was, an old workingman. What a horror that he should be seen this way by passing strangers, or by his own grandson!

So he watched, and one morning he did see a group of school children coming up the aisle. Without having to look closely, Frank knew that his solemn, black-haired grandson was in this third-grade expedition and that his sharp eyes would be darting here and there, seeking the grandpa of whom he was so proud.

If Frank stood his ground, Donnie would see his grandpa as he had never seen him before — a dirty, tired man among many other dirty, tired men, one of thousands; not powerful, not exceptional, no more responsible than the least of them for the shining marvels that rolled off the final assembly line; different from the rest only in that he was older and more whipped than most.

Frank glanced around quickly to see that Buster was not watching, stuck his file and sandpaper halfway into the open ventilator pipe of his car, and scuttled across the aisle. There a ten-foot-high stack of station-wagon doors gave him shelter. Sweating with anxiety, Frank passed his dirty handkerchief across his wet forehead. He could have groaned aloud from shame as he peered cautiously around the edge of the stacked doors, searching for little Donnie in the knot of babbling boys and girls. He was easy to find. Far in the rear, he hunted worriedly, almost stealthily, ignoring everyone as he looked for his grandpa in all this glamorous, clamorous profusion. His head cocked now to the right and now to the left, he peered down low and he stood on his tiptoes; even as he stared, the confidence was fading from his searching, pointed little face. How often they had played this game together, laughing and panting from closet to closet, from bush to tree! But always before this Frank had allowed himself to be caught, chuckling behind a garment bag, or to have his big fat rump slapped because it stuck out from the lilac bush. Now, for the first time, he was desperate not to be discovered.

"If it isn't old Frank!"

His heart gave a great lurch. He whirled clumsily in the narrow space and confronted a man as heavy as he, with an underbite like a bulldog and a short, steaming pipe clenched between his teeth. He wore the loud yellow shirt of the union committeemen, with his name, LOU, embroidered in black above the breast pocket.

"What're you so nervous about? Don't you remember me?"

"Yes, sure, of course." It came back to him as he spoke. "You used to be a door fitter back in the old days." Frank added quickly, to forestall further questions, "I was surprised that you remembered *me*. How long have you been a committeeman?" He glanced over his shoulder. The third-graders had passed on, and Donnie was disappearing from view.

"I heard you were back in the shop. That's part of my job, I've been a plant committeeman five years now. I was vice-president once before that. It beats working. Besides, it's satisfying to help the boys out. Say, did they take the ten-dollar initiation fee out of your pay check yet, Frank?"

"Last week."

"Bring in the check stub. Any former member in good standing that comes back is entitled to have it refunded. You're supposed to turn in your withdrawal card with it, but what the hell, back in those days we were just organized. Besides, I'll vouch for you, I used to see you at meetings."

Frank stepped out into the aisle with this man whom he remembered as one of the agitators whose militancy had driven him out of the factory and into the business world where you depended only on your own personal strength.

Fortunately the line had slowed almost to a stop, and his job, with his file jutting out of it, stood not far from them. He wiped his palms on his dungarees and accepted Lou's clean hand. "That's very kind of you."

"Ten bucks is ten bucks. They're expecting me over in Labor Relations, we're processing a hot grievance. Don't forget that stub, Frank." Lou clapped him on the back and was gone in a cloud of plumed blue smoke.

Frank felt confused. As he bent grimly to his work, feeling the folds of flesh protesting, he was sick with a double guilt at hiding from Donnie and at encountering Lou; but if he had somehow reversed it — if he had stepped out and hailed his little grandson, and then hidden from the union official — wouldn't he have felt just as guilty?

The fact was that they had sought him out, both of them, when he had wanted above everything to remain forgotten and alone. It made him wonder, gnawingly, whether maybe May wasn't right, whether he wasn't attempting the impossible, crawling into this noisy, dirty hole and pulling the lid down over his head. But what else could I have done? he asked himself. Could I have opened a hole-in-the-wall candy store and made half what I'm making now, with nothing at the end of the road to show for the endless hours and the swollen feet? He had a sudden vision of himself waiting for trade behind the counter of a failing store, of May in the back room where the stale stock was stored, heating him a pot of coffee over a single burner, of Donnie and Jerry coming in to get free candy, of Ray slipping him an envelope containing rent money that he could hardly spare.

No, he said to himself, no matter how much Ray is ashamed of me now, at least he doesn't have to support me. The thought swelled in him like the satisfaction of a good deed, and as it spread it crowded out the less agreeable thoughts one by one until he grew to feel that no one else had fully recognized the act of courage involved in going back to this life. He resolved that he would hide from no one any more.

That night Donnie called him on the telephone.

"Grandpa, we went through the factory today and I looked all over for you, but I couldn't find you."

"I know, sonny. I saw you, but I couldn't come over to you. I work pretty hard there." Frank looked up into his wife's eyes.

"I figured you did. I told my friends you were in conference."

Frank hesitated. "Where'd you hear that? Your father say that?"

"No, Daddy told me you were there like all those other men, but I thought he was kidding."

"He wasn't kidding. I work just like everybody else. I have to, in order to take care of Grandma and me, so we'll have money for when we get old." He considered for an instant, then laughed and said, "I mean *real* old."

When he had hung up, he shuffled back to his three-way

chair and eased himself onto it like a man leaning back for a barber shave. His wife patted him as she passed.

"So that's how it goes," she said mildly.

"Why not? If I'm going to be there ten years we all might as well start to get used to it. I wasn't ashamed of working during those first eleven years I was there, was I? So why should I be now?"

"Nobody ever said," May replied in her familiar shorthand. He was satisfied.

And besides, he thought, although he did not know quite how to put it into words, perhaps he belonged in the factory even more now than he had as a young man. Because now he was no longer young and neither was the factory, although it was new. Fewer and fewer laborers would be needed as the years went by and automation proceeded; the work would be less and less physically demanding; and he could even foresee dimly, as one half-believingly envisions one's children full of years, a time when the factory would be one vast, echoing cavern, the moving lines, belts, pulleys, and conveyors doing their tasks unaided by human sweat, only tended here and there by a besmocked, unsoiled technician, keen and watchful. Who more logical to observe this gradual depopulation, this slow disappearance of the working class, than he himself, the prodigal who had returned to make his peace with the factory world? . . . Meantime, however, the drudgery remained.

Before he and May turned in, he riffled through the papers in the desk drawer until he found the stub of his pay check, and he transferred it to the wallet in his work pants.

The next day was payday. Trying to calculate what would be coming to him after all the deductions, Frank remembered bitterly the taut expectancy with which he used to check out his cash register and add up the cash receipts.

"Always like this on payday," muttered Pop, the old inspector. "Too many men, not enough work for everybody!"

Frank looked at him uneasily. "What do you mean, too many men?"

"There's so many guys knock off one or two days a week to look for other work, the only way the company can pull production is to hire more than they need. But then when everybody shows up on payday, they got too many."

How different from the old days! But didn't it prove that none of the absentees were any more satisfied than he with what they did, that in the end all of them were united by one bond and one bond only: the pay check?

But he had alighted for good, to serve out his term perched here like an old bird, while they, so much younger, were still flapping their wings, still taking trial flights to see if there was some place else they could land, some work place that would sustain them better than this.

Had he really acquired the courage of renunciation, the kind of courage you needed when you got older? He was startled by the approach of Buster, rags and can of naphtha in hand.

"Here, Frank," the foreman said, "never mind that metal-finishing. I've got an extra metal finisher as it is. Soak these rags and wipe the whole panel clean on every job, then scrub it up and down, you know how, to bring out the high lights. They want the metal finishers to be able to see what they're working on."

Frank shrugged. The indeterminate They, the planners and the engineers, were always devising more exhausting ways to do a dull job — it was one means of justifying their existence.

It also meant that he was expendable. Panting as he labored, Frank assured himself, They wouldn't do that, they wouldn't pull that on me. What he meant was, although he could hardly dare to put it into words: Not after what I've swallowed these last few weeks, in here, on the street, from my friends, even from my family.

But Buster approached again and stood watching him. Frank sensed that he was going to say something; waiting and working, he could bear it no longer. His face red, the vein in his temple pounding, he spoke without straightening up from his work.

"This is miserable work," he said tensely.

"You might as well leave off." Buster used his tongue to shift his cigar. "They want you over by the body shop office."

"Now?"

"Yes." Buster turned quickly and walked away, as if afraid that he would be asked why.

Frank put down the dirty rags and the sandpaper block and walked down the aisle and over another aisle to the body shop office. A dozen men were gathered in front of it, in the red-and-yellow-striped smoking area. Several stood with folded arms; two squatted on their haunches like soldiers planning strategy with their fingertips in the dust; three leaned pensively against the glass partition that boxed in the office from the factory noises; one sat withdrawn on the red fireplug with his legs crossed, fingering a cigarette and muttering to himself. A leaner, a man who had been hired at the same time as Frank, gave him a nod of recognition.

"They tapped you too, eh?"

Frank raised his eyebrows. "What's up?"

"We're getting laid off, that's what. All of us." The man laughed angrily. "I'd like to know what the hell they hired us for if they didn't need us."

"But . . . " Frank stopped helplessly. There was nothing to say.

A smooth-faced boy nudged him frankly. "Say, pop, haven't *you* got seniority?"

He shook his head wordlessly.

"You haven't been here ninety days either?"

He shook his head again. He felt alone and naked. He was no closer to these fellow victims than he was to the masked men just across the aisle who carefully ignored them because they still had their spotwelding guns and their jobs.

They waited together sullenly for an hour, perhaps less,

perhaps more — Frank did not draw out his pocket watch. He knew only, as he stood silently amid the curses around him, that he had descended like a skin diver past all the other sunken wrecks of his fifty-six-year plunge through the waters of his destiny until he had struck bottom. There had been the bland bankers' faces of the comfortable men who had refused him credit; there had been the depression faces of the harried women who had refused to buy his tableware; there had been the averted faces of his son and nephew, fearing that he would ask them for money, hoping despite their shame that he would cling to this job like a sea gull to a rock. But now there were no more faces for him to use as mirrors. He stood on the ocean floor, the breath gone from his lungs, his brain pleading uselessly for oxygen.

What do I tell Donnie now, he wondered, now that I have started with the truth? Do I go on with it and explain to an eight-year-old how it feels to be fired — kicked out and flung aside at fifty-six? Or do I consult first with his parents about their modern psychology of handling problems like jobless Grandpa — and so plead without words, Ray, my son, my son, help me?

The yellow shirt of Lou the committeeman flashed past him. And stopped. Lou turned, his hand on the doorknob of the body shop office.

"Hi, Frank," he said. "You bring in that check stub for me?"

Frank fumbled with the button on his blue work shirt and at last brought forth the stub from his wallet.

"That's it. I'll take care — say, wait a minute. What you doing here with these guys?"

Frank lifted his shoulders. He swallowed. "Buster told me to report here. Getting laid off, I guess."

"The hell you say." Lou drew back as though he had been told something disgusting. "Wait right here." He plunged into the office, where he at once encountered Hawks, the body shop superintendent. His jaw was working and his finger pointing, but it was impossible to hear a sound through the glass. The two of them, their mouths moving, retreated under the fluorescents until they had gained the privacy of a partitioned office.

Fascinated, jealous, brought back to life, the discarded and forgotten men clustered around him. "How come he knows you?" "You think he can fix it up?" "What's your secret, dad?"

His hands trembling, Frank said, "Honestly, I don't —" but then they all saw Lou and the sad-faced superintendent coming towards the door again. The committeeman stuck his head out the door and said abruptly: "Frank."

He stepped forward. Mesmerized, he looked up from the dazzling tie on the superintendent's breast to the disconsolate and permanently disappointed face. It opened in a brief, glacial smile and then closed again. "You used to work here."

Frank stared into the man's dead, expressionless eyes. "I put in eleven years."

"Go on over to Vernon, the foreman next to the jigs. Tell

him I said to give you something for the rest of the day." He turned his back and walked to a telephone, scratching between the cheeks of his behind as he walked, ignoring the faces that watched him through the glass.

Blinking, Frank suddenly realized that Lou was winking at him. "Go on," the committeeman said in a friendly way, "finish out the day with Vernon. After that we'll see, all right?"

Frank nodded — he could find no words — and started to go.

"And say, Frank." Lou waited until Frank had turned to face him. "You're coming to the union picnic tomorrow, aren't you?"

"Why, I hadn't — "

"Twentieth anniversary, all the old gang'll be there. Bring the kiddies — we'll have rides, eats, the works." He waved and was gone.

Vernon gave Frank a can of red primer and a brush. "Paint around the ventilator pipe and inside the gas-tank door at the back."

For the rest of the day Frank circled the swinging steel bodies, dabbing and daubing and wondering what to do when he got home. He had still not decided when the siren blew and he took his shuffling place in line at the time clock. Tensely he moved forward until he could see his own card in the rack. No pink card, as he had half expected — and as there were, scattered here and there through the rack — saying: DO NOT PUNCH THIS. BRING IT TO THE

OFFICE. He took out his old card from the slot, punched it, and went home.

May was baking. He entered, sniffing, and was caught up in a sudden feeling of love for her as she advanced, wiping her plump, floury hands on her apron and pouting for a kiss.

"How's everything, Daddy?"

He evaded by demanding, "What do I smell?"

"Apple pie. The apples Ray brought are so good I hated to think of them going to waste."

When they had finished dinner, Frank told her what had happened without trying to explain to her how he had felt. At the end he said, "So there's this picnic. There's no place I want to go less, but I feel obliged to show up on account of Lou's going to bat for me."

"We could take Donnie and Jerry, they'd love it. Why don't you want to go?"

Frank stared at his wife, dismayed. "How does it look, my hanging around those labor people at my age? You know I was never hot for the union. Then supposing Monday comes — and I get laid off? They'll think I came purposely to save my job, to show my face and get in good."

"They wouldn't think that about you. People can tell what you are by your face, Frank."

There was already a great crowd when Frank and May arrived at the picnic grounds, Frank holding Donnie by the hand, May carrying Jerry. Tags were pinned to them all, and Frank, labeled and lost, wished with all his heart that he were locked in his living room with the TV; but then the boys spotted the jelly-apple stand, and the day was turned over to them at last, in Frank's mind as well as in fact.

He and May split up to take the children on different rides. His own separateness from the other picnickers seemed unimportant as he watched Donnie's face turn red and white with awful glee as he clutched the rail of his dodgem car. While he stood alone in the sawdust, craning his neck and shouting encouragement to Donnie, a stranger wearing one of the yellow committeeman shirts tapped him on the shoulder. "Say, brother, do you admit to being fifty?"

Frank felt the blood coming to his face. "I'm more than that, I guess anybody can tell."

The man laughed aloud, showing two missing canines. "No offense," he said in a beery voice. "We got to round up enough men for our Cover Boy contest. That's the only regulation, you got to be over fifty."

Frank said quickly, "Oh, but I don't want to —"

"Come on, be a sport. It's all in fun, and there's going to be prizes for the winners."

"I really don't —"

Donnie had scrambled out of the car and threw himself immediately into the conversation. "What don't you want, Grandpa? What?"

The committeeman took advantage of the boy's eagerness. "We want your Grandpa to enter a contest, and maybe win a prize."

So of course he went to the main bandstand with Donnie and the committeeman. A pigeon-breasted woman, wearing a union overseas cap askew on her freshly permanented gray curls and a broad golden sash lettered LADIES' AUX-ILIARY, took his name for her clipboard and jerked her thumb over her shoulder. What an old fool I am, Frank thought wearily, as he mounted the rickety steps of the bandstand and sat down with a group of older men, one or two of whom he recognized, at the right of the union's marching band.

The woman had seated Donnie down in the front row. Sinking his new grown-up teeth fiercely into his jelly apple, Donnie waved to his Grandpa and cocked his feet up. Before he fully understood what was going on, Frank was being led across the stage in front of the musicians; a scatter of applause rose in volume as he crossed the boards. Surprised, he looked out past his cheering grandson. All the empty rows were being filled with members and their wives, many of whom were clapping vigorously for him.

"Say, what is this?" he demanded, his ears burning, and turned to see an arm being held above his head with a numbered card.

Oh my God, he thought miserably, they're making fun of me. He shrank down wretchedly into the collar of his sport jacket, but the crowd, seeing his embarrassment, began to clap all the louder. As he stood there, he was joined one by

one by the other contestants, facing all of the shouting,
laughing throng of their fellow workers. The master of cer-
emonies held his card above the head of each in turn, demanding a verdict in applause.

It was a blur to Frank — the noise, the whistles, the
laughter, the rattling drums. He thought he heard voices
shouting, "Hey, Frankie! Frankie boy!" but he was not certain whether they were calling to him or to someone else.
Rubbing his sweating palms up and down on his hips, he
looked about like a trapped animal. A sharp-nosed old gaf-
fer from the material-handling department, who had been
playing up to the crowd, was being presented with a small
silver loving cup — he had already been awarded first prize
in the Cover Boy contest.

Frank was next. As he wiped his hand across his face un-
believingly, he looked down to see a box of cigars being
thrust toward him.

"The second prize winner, Frank, the handsomest man
in the body shop, and a real good sport!"

"No, no, I really can't," Frank started to say, but everyone was crowding around him and clapping him on the
back, the band was playing, and out on the grass beyond
Donnie, who was jumping up and down and waving his
jelly apple, was May with Jerry on her shoulder. No one
was ridiculing him, he realized at last — everyone was being simply friendly.

As Frank approached his wife and his grandsons, he was
intercepted by Lou the committeeman, his pipe streaming

clouds of smoke in the afternoon air. "Been looking all over for you."

"I sort of got shanghaied into this thing."

"What the hell, you can always smoke the cigars. Listen, I got Salvatore, the vice-president, to talk to Hawks last night after work. He agreed to pull your name off the lay-off list."

"But . . ." Frank stopped and stared stupidly at Lou. "How could he make Hawks do that?"

"Make him, it isn't a question of make him. We got no legal right. But they got to live with us like we got to live with them. Sal said it wasn't right, knocking off a man with eleven years, even though you been away and lost your seniority. And Hawks finally broke down and agreed. So the job's yours, Frank. It's not the greatest job in the world, you probably had better these last years, but now that you're back in the saddle again . . . Once you get your ninety days in, it's yours for as long as you want it."

Holding the cigars awkwardly, Frank looked up, his eyes swimming, into his wife's smiling face.

"This is my committeeman, May," he said to her. "He says I'm not going to get laid off after all."

May transferred little Jerry, sticky and yawning, to his outstretched arms. "You've got a mighty nice crowd here," she said. "Frank never did tell me just how nice they were." As the committeeman waved his hand in farewell, she tousled Donnie's hair and turned to her husband. "Let's go play bingo with the kids, Frank, maybe we can win a set of dishes. I think this is our lucky day."

Hand in hand, enfolding their grandchildren, who were now more tired than they, they strolled leisurely through the friendly throng toward the last little victory of the waning afternoon.

APPENDIX

The Myth of
the Happy Worker

"From where we sit in the company," says one of the best
personnel men in the country, "we have to look at only the
aspects of work that cut across all sorts of jobs—administration
and human relations. Now these are aspects of work, abstrac-
tions, but it's easy for personnel people to get so hipped on
their importance that they look on the specific tasks of making
things and selling them as secondary. . . ."

— *The Organization Man*
William H. Whyte, Jr.

The personnel man who made this remark to Mr. Whyte
differed from his brothers only in that he had a moment of
insight. Actually, "the specific tasks of making things" are
now not only regarded by his white-collar fellows as "secondary," but as irrelevant to the vaguer but more "chal-

lenging" tasks of the man at the desk. This is true not just of the personnel man, who places workers, replaces them, displaces them—in brief, manipulates them. The union leader also, who represents workers and sometimes manipulates them, seems increasingly to regard what his workers do as merely subsidiary to the job he himself is doing in the larger community. This job may be building the Red Cross or the Community Chest, or it may sometimes be—as the Senate hearings suggest—participating in such communal endeavors as gambling, prostitution and improving the breed. In any case, the impression is left that the problems of the workers in the background (or underground) have been stabilized, if not permanently solved.

With the personnel man and the union leader, both of whom presumably see the worker from day to day, growing so far away from him, it is hardly to be wondered at that the middle-class in general, and articulate middle-class intellectuals in particular, see the worker vaguely, as through a cloud. One gets the impression that when they do consider him, they operate from one of two unspoken assumptions: (1) The worker has died out like the passenger pigeon, or is dying out, or becoming accultured, like the Navajo; (2) If he *is* still around, he is just like the rest of us—fat, satisfied, smug, a little restless, but hardly distinguishable from his fellow TV-viewers of the middle-class.

Lest it be thought that (1) is somewhat exaggerated, I hasten to quote from a recently-published article apparently dedicated to the laudable task of urging slothful middle-class intellectuals to wake up and live: "The old-style sweatshop crippled mainly the working people. Now there are no workers left in America; we are almost all middle-class as to income and expectations." I do not believe the writer meant to state—although he comes perilously close to it—that nobody works anymore. If I understand him correctly, he is referring to the fact that the worker's rise in real income over the last decade, plus the diffusion of middle-class tastes and values throughout a large part of the underlying population, has made it increasingly difficult to tell blue-collar from white-collar worker without a program. In short, if the worker earns like the middle-class, votes like the middle-class, dresses like the middle-class, dreams like the middle-class, then he ceases to exist as a worker.

But there is one thing that the worker doesn't do like the middle-class: he works like a worker. The steel-mill puddler does not yet sort memos, the coal miner does not yet sit in conferences, the cotton millhand does not yet sip martinis from his lunchbox. The worker's attitude toward his work is generally compounded of hatred, shame and resignation.

Before I spell out what I think this means, I should like first to examine some of the implications of the widely-held belief that "we are almost all middle-class as to income and expectations." I am neither economist, sociologist nor politician, and I hold in my hand no doctored statistics to be haggled over. I am by profession a writer who has had occasion to work in factories at various times during the Thirties, Forties and Fifties. The following observations are simply impressions based on my last period of factory servitude, in 1956.

The average automobile worker gets a little better than two dollars an hour. As such he is one of the best-paid factory workers in the country. After twenty years of militant struggle led by the union that I believe to be still the finest and most democratic labor organization in the United States, hc is earning less than the starting salaries offered to inexperienced and often semi-literate college graduates without dependents. After compulsory deductions for taxes, social security, old-age insurance and union dues, and optional deductions for hospitalization and assorted charities, his paycheck for forty hours of work is going to be closer to seventy than to eighty dollars a week. Does this make him middle-class as to income? Does it rate with the weekly take of a dentist, an accountant, a salesman, a draftsman, a journalist? Surely it would be more to the point to ask how a family man can get by in the Fifties on that kind of income. I know how he does it, and I should think the answers would be a little disconcerting to those who wax glib on the satisfactory status of the "formerly" underprivileged.

For one thing, he works a lot longer than forty hours a week—when he can. Since no automobile company is as yet in a position to guarantee its workers anything like fifty weeks of steady forty-hour paychecks, the auto worker knows he has to make it while he can. During peak production periods he therefore puts in nine, ten, eleven and often twelve hours a day on the assembly line for weeks on end. And that's not all. If he has dependents, as like as not he also holds down a "spare-time" job. I have worked on the line with men who doubled as mechanics, repairmen, salesmen, contractors, builders, farmers, cab-drivers, lumberyard workers, countermen. I would guess that there are many more of these than show up in the official statistics: often a man will work for less if he can be paid under the counter with tax-free dollars.

Nor is that all. The factory worker with dependents cannot carry the debt load he now shoulders—the middle-class debt load, if you like, of nagging payments on car, washer, dryer, TV, clothing, house itself—without family help. Even if he puts in fifty, sixty or seventy hours a week at one or two jobs, he has to count on his wife's paycheck, or his son's, his daughter's, his brother-in-law's; or on his mother's social security, or his father's veteran's pension. The working-class family today is not typically held together by the male wage-earner, but by multiple wage-earners often of several generations who club together to get the things they want and need—or are pressured into believing they must have. It is at best a precarious arrangement; as for its toll on the physical organism and the psyche, that is a question perhaps worthy of further investigation by those who currently pronounce themselves bored with Utopia Unlimited in the Fat Fifties.

But what of the worker's middle-class expectations? I had been under the impression that this was the rock on which Socialist agitation had foundered for generations: it proved useless to tell the proletarian that he had a world to win when he was reasonably certain that with a few breaks he could have his own gas station. If these expectations have changed at all in recent years, they would seem to have narrowed rather than expanded, leaving a psychological increment of resignation rather than of unbounded optimism (except among the very young—and even among them the optimism focuses more often on better-paying opportunities elsewhere in the labor market than on illusory hopes of swift status advancement). The worker's expectations are for better pay, more humane working conditions, more job security. As long as he feels that he is going to achieve them through an extension of existing conditions, for that long he is going to continue to be a middle-class conservative in temper. But only for that long.

I suspect that what middle-class writers mean by the worker's middle-class expectations are his cravings for commodities—his determination to have not only fin-tailed cars and single-unit washer-dryers, but butterfly chairs in the rumpus room, African masks on the wall and power boats in the garage. Before the middle-class intellectuals condemn these expectations too harshly, let them consider, first, who has been utilizing every known technique of suasion and propaganda to convert luxuries into necessities, and second, at what cost these new necessities are acquired by the American working-class family.

Now I should like to return to the second image of the American worker: satisfied, doped by TV, essentially middle-class in outlook. This is an image bred not of communication with workers (except as mediated by hired interviewers sent "into the field" like anthropologists or entomologists), but of contempt for people, based perhaps on self-contempt and on a feeling among intellectuals that the worker has let them down. In order to see this clearly, we have to place it against the intellectual's changing attitudes toward the worker since the Thirties.

At the time of the organization of the C.I.O., the middle-class intellectual saw the proletarian as society's figure of virtue—heroic, magnanimous, bearing in his loins the seeds of a better future; he would have found ludicrous the suggestion that a sit-down striker might harbor anti-Semitic feelings. After Pearl Harbor, the glamorization of the worker was taken over as a function of government. Then, however, he was no longer the builder of the future good society; instead he was second only to the fighting man as the vital winner of the war. Many intellectuals, as government employees, found themselves helping to create this new portrait of the worker as patriot.

But in the decade following the war intellectuals have discovered that workers are no longer either building socialism or forging the tools of victory. All they are doing is making the things that other people buy. That, and participating in the great commodity scramble. The disillusionment, it would seem, is almost too terrible to bear. Word has gotten around among the highbrows that the worker is not heroic or idealistic; public-opinion polls prove that he wants barbecue pits more than foreign aid and air-condi-

tioning more than desegregation, that he doesn't particularly
want to go on strike, that he is reluctant to form a Labor
Party, that he votes for Stevenson and often even for Eisen-
hower and Nixon—that he is, in short, animated by the
same aspirations as drive the middle-class onward and up-
ward in suburbia.

There is of course a certain admixture of self-delusion in
the middle-class attitude that workers are now the same as
everybody else. For me it was expressed most precisely last
year in the dismay and sympathy with which middle-class
friends greeted the news that I had gone back to work in a
factory. If workers are now full-fledged members of the middle-class, why the dismay? What difference whether one sits
in an office or stands in a shop? The answer is so obvious
that one feels shame at laboring the point. But I have news
for my friends among the intellectuals. The answer is obvious
to workers, too.

They know that there is a difference between working with
your back and working with your behind (I do not make
the distinction between hand-work and brain-work, since we
are all learning that white-collar work is becoming less and
less brain-work). They know that they work harder than the
middle-class for less money. Nor is it simply a question of
status, that magic word so dear to the hearts of the socio-
logues, the new anatomizers of the American corpus. It is
not simply status-hunger that makes a man hate work which
pays *less* than other work he knows about, if *more* than any
other work he has been trained for (the only reason my

fellow-workers stayed on the assembly line, they told me again and again). It is not simply status-hunger that makes a man hate work that is mindless, endless, stupefying, sweaty, filthy, noisy, exhausting, insecure in its prospects and practically without hope of advancement.

The plain truth is that factory work is degrading. It is degrading to any man who ever dreams of doing something worthwhile with his life; and it is about time we faced the fact. The more a man is exposed to middle-class values, the more sophisticated he becomes and the more production-line work is degrading to him. The immigrant who slaved in the poorly-lighted, foul, vermin-ridden sweatshop found his work less degrading than the native-born high school graduate who reads Judge Parker, Rex Morgan, M.D., and Judd Saxon, Business Executive, in the funnies, and works in a fluorescent factory with ticker-tape production-control machines. For the immigrant laborer, even the one who did not dream of socialism, his long hours were going to buy him freedom. For the factory worker of the Fifties, his long hours are going to buy him commodities . . . and maybe reduce a few of his debts.

Almost without exception, the men with whom I worked on the assembly line last year felt like trapped animals. Depending on their age and personal circumstances, they were either resigned to their fate, furiously angry at *themselves* for what they were doing, or desperately hunting other work that would pay as well and in addition offer some variety, some prospect of change and betterment. They were sick of being pushed around by harried foremen (themselves more pitied than hated), sick of working like blinkered donkeys, sick of being dependent for their livelihood on a maniacal production-merchandising setup, sick of working in a place where there was no spot to relax during the twelve-minute rest period. (Someday—let us hope—we will marvel that production was still so worshipped in the Fifties that new factories could be built with every splendid facility for the storage and movement of essential parts, but with no place for a resting worker to sit down for a moment but on a fire plug, the edge of a packing case, or the sputum- and oil-stained stairway of a toilet.)

The older men stay put and wait for their vacations. But since the assembly line demands young blood (you will have a hard time getting hired if you are over thirty-five), the factory in which I worked was aswarm with new faces every day; labor turnover was so fantastic and absenteeism so rampant, with the young men knocking off a day of two every week to hunt up other jobs, that the company was forced to over-hire in order to have sufficient workers on hand at the starting siren.

To those who will object—fortified by their readings in C. Wright Mills and A. C. Spectorsky—that the white-collar commuter, too, dislikes his work, accepts it only because it buys his family commodities, and is constantly on the prowl for other work, I can only reply that for me at any rate this is proof not of the disappearance of the working-class but of the proletarianization of the middle-class. Perhaps it is not taking place quite in the way that Marx envisaged it, but the alienation of the white-collar man (like that of the laborer) from both his tools and whatever he produces, the slavery that chains the exurbanite to the commuting time-table (as the worker is still chained to the time-clock), the anxiety that sends the white-collar man home with his brief-case for an evening's work (as it degrades the workingman into pleading for long hours of overtime), the displacement of the white-collar slum from the wrong side of the tracks to the suburbs (just as the working-class slum is moved from old-law tenements to skyscraper barracks)—all these mean to me that the white-collar man is entering (though his arms may be loaded with commodities) the grey world of the working man.

Three quotations from men with whom I worked may help to bring my view into focus:

Before starting work: "Come on, suckers, they say the Foundation wants to give away *more* than half a billion this year. Let's do and die for the old Foundation."

During rest period: "Ever stop to think how we crawl here bumper to bumper, and crawl home bumper to bumper, and we've got to turn out more every minute to keep our jobs, when there isn't even any room for them on the highways?"

At quitting time (this from older foremen, whose job is not only to keep things moving, but by extension to serve as company spokesmen): "You're smart to get out of here. ... I curse the day I ever started, now I'm struck: any man with brains that stays here ought to have his head examined. This is no place for an intelligent human being."

Such is the attitude towards the work. And towards the product? On the one hand it is admired and desired as a symbol of freedom, almost a substitute for freedom, not because the worker participated in making it, but because our whole culture is dedicated to the proposition that the automobile is both necessary and beautiful. On the other hand it is hated and despised—so much that if your new car smells bad it may be due to a banana peel crammed down its gullet and sealed up thereafter, so much so that if your dealer can't locate the rattle in your new car you might ask him to open the welds on one of those tailfins and vacuum out the nuts and bolts thrown in by workers sabotaging their own product.

Sooner or later, if we want a decent society—by which I do not mean a society glutted with commodities or one maintained in precarious equilibrium by over-buying and forced premature obsolescence—we are going to have to come face to face with the problem of work. Apparently the Russians have committed themselves to the replenishment of their labor force through automatic recruitment of those intellectually incapable of keeping up with severe scholastic requirements in the public educational system. Apparently we, too, are heading in the same direction: although our economy is not directed, and although college education is as yet far from free, we seem to be operating in this capitalist economy on the totalitarian assumption that we can funnel the underprivileged, undereducated, or just plain undere-quipped, into the factory, where we can proceed to forget about them once we have posted the minimum fair labor standards on the factory wall.

If this is what we want, let's be honest enough to say so. If we conclude that there is nothing noble about repetitive work, but that it is nevertheless good enough for the lower orders, let's say that, too, so we will at least know where we stand. But if we cling to the belief that other men are our brothers, not just Egyptians, or Israelis, or Hungarians, but *all* men, including millions of Americans who grind their lives away on an insane treadmill, then we will have to start thinking about how their work and their lives can be made meaningful. That is what I assume the Hungarians, both workers and intellectuals, have been thinking about. Since no one has been ordering us what to think, since no one has been forbidding our intellectuals to fraternize with our workers, shouldn't it be a little easier for us to admit, first, that our problems exist, then to state them, and then to see if we can resolve them?